Lawrie Ryan

Top Chemistry Grades for You

GCSE Revision Guide for AQA Co-ordinated

Contents

What do you call a lot of parrots joined together?

Poly-parrot

Revision Calendar (detachable, for your bedroom wall)

Revision Cards (detachable, for revision in spare moments)

To see the latest Exam Specification for AQA Co-ordinated Science, visit **www.aqa.org.uk**

To see this Exam Specification 'mapped' with the relevant pages in *Chemistry for You*, visit **www.chemistryforyou.co.uk**

Introduction

Top Chemistry Grades for You is designed to help you achieve the best possible grades in your GCSE examination.

It focuses on exactly what you need to do to succeed in the AQA Coordinated Science exam (for Single or for Double Award, and at either Foundation or Higher Tier), or in the AQA Chemistry B exam.

There is a separate book for AQA Modular Science and AQA Modular Chemistry.

This revision book is best used together with the **Chemistry for You** textbook, but it can also be used by itself.

There are also books for
Top Biology Grades for You and
Top Physics Grades for You.

For each section in the AQA Coordinated Science examination specification, there is a Topic as shown on the opposite page.

For each Topic there are 2 double-page spreads:

- a **Revision** spread, which shows you exactly what you need to know (see below), and

- a **Questions** spread, which lets you try out some exam questions on this topic.
  The **Answers** for these, with Examiners' Tips, are given at the back of the book.

In addition, for each section of Topics there is:

- a **Sample Answer** spread, showing you answers at Grade-A level and at Grade-C level, with Examiners' Comments and Tips. These will help you to focus on how to improve, to move up to a higher grade.

Each Revision spread is laid out clearly, using boxes:

Each spread starts with some 'ThinkAbout' questions, to help you focus on the topic. The answers are shown at the bottom of the page.

Topic number.

The pages show essential content for the exam.

Items are often boxed for clarity.

Boxes marked **D** are needed for Double Science (and for Triple Science). These are not needed for Single-Award Science.

Boxes marked **H** are needed for the Higher Tier only. These are not needed for the Foundation Tier.

Answers to the 'ThinkAbout' questions are given here.

Page references for more details, if you need them.

A 'Take care' box of Examiners' Tips.

As a first step, go through this book and:

- If you are studying for Single-Award Science, cross out all the boxes labelled **D**

- If you are studying for the Foundation Tier, cross out all the boxes labelled **H**

- If you are **not** studying for Triple Award Chemistry, cross out all of Topics 16, 17, 18, 19.

Then use the pull-out **Revision Calendar** to keep a record of your progress.

At the back of the book there are detachable **Revision Cards**, with very brief summaries. You can use these to top up your revision in spare moments – for example, when sitting on a bus or waiting for a lesson.

Best wishes for a great result in your exams.

Lawrie Ryan

Revision Technique

Prepare

1. Go through the book, crossing out any boxes that you don't need (as described at the bottom of page 3).

2. While doing this, you can decide which are your strong topics, and which topics you need to spend more time on.

3. You need to balance your time between:
   - **Revising** what you need to know about Chemistry. To do this, use the first double-page spread in each topic.
   - **Practising** by doing exam questions. To do this, use the second spread in each topic.

   Do these two things for each topic in turn.

Revise

4. Think about your best ways of revising. Some of the best ways are to do something *active*. To use active learning you can:
   - Write down **notes**, as a summary of the topic (while reading through the double-page spread). Use highlighter pens to colour key words.
   - Make a **poster** to summarise each topic (and pin it up on your bedroom wall?). Make it colourful, and use images/sketches if you can.
   - Make a spider-diagram or **mind map** of each topic. See the example here, but use your own style:
   - Ask someone (family or friend) to **test** you on the topic.
   - **Teach** the topic to someone (family or friend).

   Which method works best for you?

5. It is usually best to work in a quiet room, for about 25–30 minutes at a time, and then take a 5–10 minute break.

6. After you have revised a topic, make a note of the date on the pull-out **Revision Calendar**.

✓ 3rd April

Practise

7. When you have revised a topic, and think you know it well, then it's important to practise it, by answering some exam questions. Turn to the second spread of the topic and answer the questions as well as you can.

8. When you have finished them, turn to the **Answers and Examiners' Tips** that start on page 92. Check your answers, and read the Examiners' Hints. Can you see how to improve your answers in future?

9. Keep a record of your progress on the **Revision Calendar**.

✓ 3rd April
✓ 4th April

Re-revise and Top-up

10. It is important to re-revise each topic again, after an interval. The best intervals are after 10 minutes, after 1 day, and after 1 week (see the graphs in *Chemistry for You*, pages 384–385).

    For this top-up you can use the topic spread, your notes, poster or mindmap, and the **Revision Cards** at the back of this book.

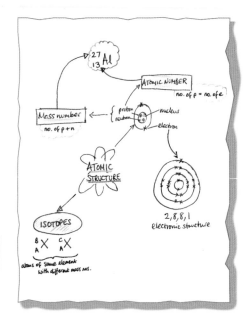

A **Mind Map** for Topic 1: Atomic Structure.

A Mind Map always makes more sense when you make it **yourself**.

Use colour and images if you can.

A revision flowchart:

Choose a topic to revise.

1. Revise

- **ThinkAbout** : try the questions in the ThinkAbout box.
  The answers are at the bottom of the page.

- **Read** the rest of the double-page spread.
  Focus on any parts you are not sure about.

- **Do** make Notes, or a Poster, or a Mind Map.
  Highlight key points in colour.

- **Re-read** the spread after a break of 5–10 minutes.

- **Take care** : read the 'Take care' box.
  Can you see how you can use this advice?

- ✓ **Tick and date** the pull-out Revision Calendar.

2. Practise

- **Try** the questions on the double-page of questions.
  These are in the same style as the ones in the exam.

- **Check** your answers. The answers begin on page 92.
  Read the Examiners' Hints carefully.
  Go back over anything you find difficult.

- ✓ **Tick and date** the pull-out Revision Calendar to
  keep a record of your progress.

Then later:

Re-visit
Re-visit each topic 1 day later, and then 1 week later.
Read the double-page spread, your notes or Mind Map,
and the questions you answered.

Up your Grade
At the end of each section of topics, read the Sample
Answers at Grade A and Grade C.
Look at the Hints and Tips for improving your grade.

Top-up
Use the Revision Cards to remind you of the key points,
and test yourself.
Even better, make your own Revision Cards.

Examination Technique

Before the exam

1. Make sure you know the dates and times of all your exams, so that you are not late!
   See the table at the bottom of this page.

2. Make sure you know which topics are going to be examined on which paper.

3. On the night before the exam, it may help to do some quick revision – but don't do too much.
   Make sure you get a good night's sleep.

On the day of the exam

1. Aim to arrive early at the exam room.

2. Make sure that you are properly equipped with pens and pencils (including spares), a rubber, a ruler, a calculator (check the battery!) and a watch.

During the exam

1. Don't waste time when you get the paper. Write your name and candidate number (unless they are already printed).
   Read the instructions on the front page of the booklet, carefully, and make sure you follow them.

2. Read each question very carefully.
   In each question there is always a 'command' word that tells you what to do.
   If the question says '*State ...*' or '*List ...*' or '*Name ...*' then you should give a short answer.
   If the question says '*Explain ...*' or '*Describe ...*' or '*Why does ...*' or '*Suggest ...*' then you should make sure you give a longer answer.

   Put a ring round each 'command' word.

   Then underline the key words in the question.
   For example:

   Then you can see exactly what is given to you in the question, and what you have to do.

   Make sure that you answer only the question shown on the exam paper (not the one that you wish had been asked).

Describe in detail what you would see when a small piece of sodium is placed in a trough of cold water.

One way of collecting information about all your exams (in all your subjects):

Date, time and room	Subject, paper number and tier	Length (hours)	Types of question: – structured? – single word answers? – longer answers? – essays?	Sections?	Details of choice (if any)	Approximate time per mark (minutes)
5th June 9.30 Hall	Science (Double Award) Paper 2 (Chemistry) Higher Tier	1½	Structured questions (with single-word answers and longer answers)	1	no choice	1 min.

Answering the questions

Structured questions

- Make sure you know *exactly* what the question is asking.

- Look for the number of marks awarded for each part of the question. For example: *(2 marks)* means that the Examiner will expect 2 main (and different) points in your answer.

- The number of lines of space is also a guide to how much you are *expected* to write.

- If there is any data provided in the question, make sure that you use it in your answer.

- Pace yourself with a watch so that you don't run out of time. You should aim to use 1 minute for each mark. So if a question has 3 marks it should take you about 3 minutes.

- In calculations, show all the steps in your working. This way you may get marks for the way you tackle the problem, even if your final answer is wrong. Make sure that you put the correct units on the answer.

- If you draw a graph, make sure that you always use more than half the grid given, and label the axes clearly. Draw the line of best fit carefully, ignoring any anomalous points.

- Try to write something for each part of *every* question.

- Follow the instructions given in the question. If it asks for one answer, give only one answer.

- If you have spare time at the end, use it wisely to check your answers.

Extended questions

- Some questions require longer answers, where you will need to write two or more full sentences.

- The questions may include the words '***Describe***...' or '***Explain***...' or '***Evaluate***...' or '***Suggest***...' or '***Why does***...'.
  For 'Explain...' you need to give *reasons* in your answer. 'Suggest...' is used when you are not expected to have learned the answer, but you should be able to write an answer using scientific principles that you know about.

- Make sure that the sentences are in good English and are linked to each other.

- Make sure you use scientific words in your answer.

- As before, the marks and the number of lines will give you a guide of how much to write. Make sure you include enough detail with at least as many points as there are marks.

- For the highest grades you need to include full details, in scientific language, written in good English, and with the sentences linking together in the correct sequence.

1

ATMIC STRUCTURE

▷ **ThinkAbout:**

1 Name the three types of sub-atomic particle found inside atoms.
2 Which of the sub-atomic particles carries a negative charge?
3 Which of the sub-atomic particles is neutral?

4 An atom has a mass number of 7 and an atomic number of 3. How many of each type of sub-atomic particle does it contain?
5 What is the difference between the atoms of isotopes of an element?

▷ **Inside atoms**

Some Ancient Greeks thought that all substances are made up from tiny particles called atoms. It was an English scientist called John Dalton, about 200 years ago, who revived this theory.

Dalton called substances that he thought contained only one type of atom 'elements'.

We have now discovered about 100 different elements.

Inside atoms we find **protons, neutrons and electrons**.

> The protons and neutrons are in the centre of the atom called the **nucleus**. This is where the mass is concentrated.

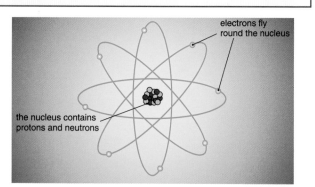

electrons fly round the nucleus

the nucleus contains protons and neutrons

Here are the properties of these sub-atomic particles:

Particle	Charge	Mass (in atomic mass units)
proton	1+	1
neutron	0	1
electron	1−	0 (almost)

D

▷ **Electronic structures**

The electrons whizz around the nucleus in **shells** (or **energy levels**).
The first shell holds up to **2** electrons.
The second shell can hold up to **8** electrons.
The third shell holds **8** electrons.

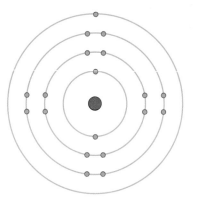

We can show an atom's **electronic structure** quickly using numbers. This tells us the arrangement of electrons around the nucleus, starting with the electrons in the innermost shell.

So, the electronic structure of a potassium atom (shown above) is 2, 8, 8, 1.

The largest atom you need to work out the electronic structure for is calcium.

Its atomic number is 20. Therefore its electronic structure is 2, 8, 8, 2.

Answers: **1** protons, neutrons, electrons **2** electrons **3** neutrons **4** It has 3 protons, 3 electrons and 4 neutrons. **5** They contain different numbers of neutrons.

8

▷ Atomic number

> The **atomic number** tells us how many protons there are in an atom.

This also equals the number of electrons. That's because atoms themselves are neutral, therefore they must have the same number of protons (+) as electrons (−).

Mass number

> The **mass number** tells us the number of protons plus neutrons.

We can show these like this:

mass number ⟶ ^{14}N
atomic number ⟶ $_7$N

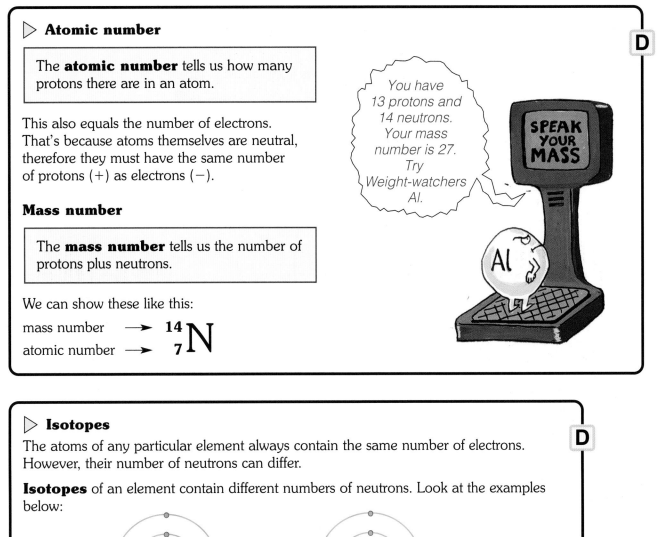

You have 13 protons and 14 neutrons. Your mass number is 27. Try Weight-watchers Al.

SPEAK YOUR MASS

▷ Isotopes

The atoms of any particular element always contain the same number of electrons. However, their number of neutrons can differ.

Isotopes of an element contain different numbers of neutrons. Look at the examples below:

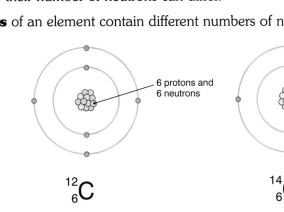

6 protons and 6 neutrons

6 protons and 8 neutrons

$^{12}_{6}$C

$^{14}_{6}$C

As you can see from this example:

> **Isotopes** of an element have the same atomic number but different mass numbers.

Isotopes are a bit like Easter eggs which have the same chocolate shell, but different numbers of sweets inside !

Take care:
The isotopes of an element undergo all the same reactions. That's because chemical properties rely on electronic structures. In isotopes of an element the arrangement of electrons is identical (see above).

More in *Chemistry for You*, pages 28–33.

Examination Questions – Atomic structure

1 a) The diagram represents an atom. Choose words from the list to label the particles.   Marks

electron   **ion**   **neutron**   **proton**

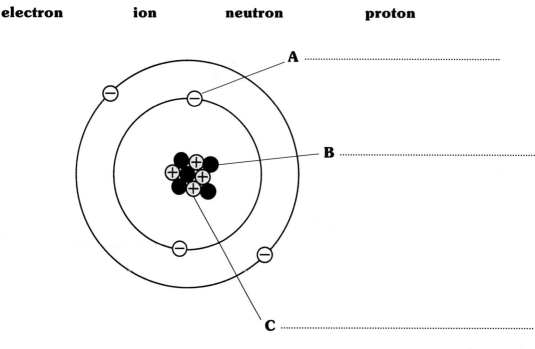

A ....

B ....

C ....

(3 marks)

b) An atom of magnesium can be represented by the symbol $^{24}_{12}$Mg.

Draw a **ring** around the letter, **A** to **D**, in the table which correctly describes the atomic structure of magnesium.

	PROTONS	ELECTRONS	NEUTRONS
A	6	6	6
B	12	12	12
C	24	12	12
D	36	12	12

(1 mark)

c) i The atomic number of aluminium is 13.
How many electrons are found in the outer shell (highest energy level) of an aluminium atom?

....

(1 mark)

ii What will be the charge on an aluminium ion?

....

(1 mark)

iii An aluminium atom contains 14 neutrons. What is its mass number?

....

(1 mark)   7

2 Use the information about a phosphorus atom to complete the table.

$$_{15}^{31}\text{P}$$

In one atom of phosphorus …

the number of protons is	a)	....
the number of neutrons is	b)	....
the number of electrons is	c)	....

3

3 a) A diagram of the nucleus of an atom is shown below.

16p
16n

  i Draw a diagram to show the electronic arrangement of this atom.

nucleus

(1 mark)

  ii What is the mass number of this atom?

....

(1 mark)

  iii Use the table on page 102 to give the chemical symbol for this element.

....

(1 mark)

  b) Name the particle in an atom that carries no overall charge.

....

(1 mark)

  c) Why is the overall charge on any atom zero?

....

....

(1 mark)

5

2 Bonding

▷ ThinkAbout:

1 Describe the movement of the particles in a solid.
2 What happens to the particles in a solid as they are warmed up?
3 What is the difference between an atom and an ion?
4 Explain what a chemical compound is.
5 Write the formula of the ions found in sodium chloride.
6 How many electrons are shared in a single covalent bond?

▷ Ionic bonding **D**

Metals bond to non-metals in **ionic compounds**. (A compound is a substance in which atoms of two, or more, elements are chemically combined.)

The metal atom gives one, or more, electrons to the non-metal atom.

This happens as the elements react together.

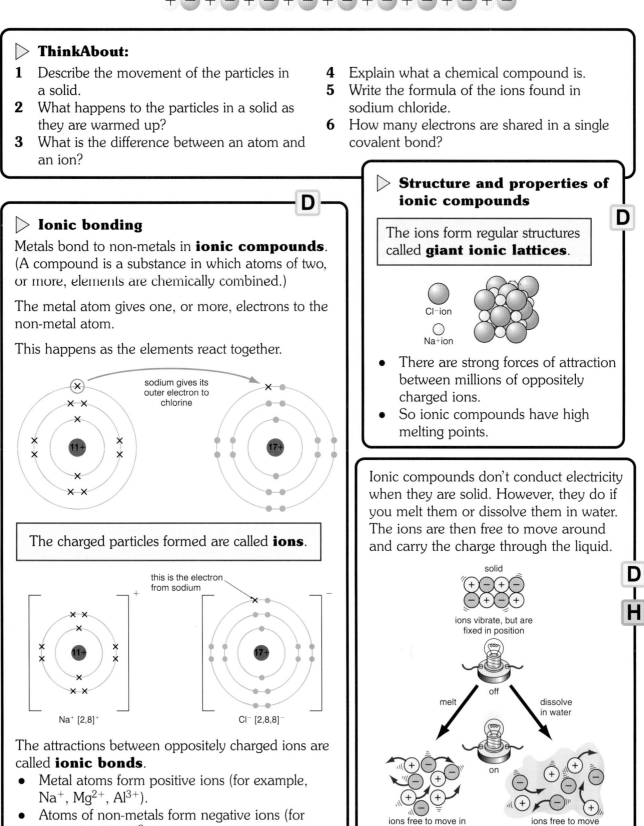

sodium gives its outer electron to chlorine

The charged particles formed are called **ions**.

this is the electron from sodium

Na$^+$ [2,8]$^+$ Cl$^-$ [2,8,8]$^-$

The attractions between oppositely charged ions are called **ionic bonds**.
- Metal atoms form positive ions (for example, Na$^+$, Mg^{2+}, Al^{3+}).
- Atoms of non-metals form negative ions (for example, Cl$^-$, O^{2-}).

▷ Structure and properties of ionic compounds **D**

The ions form regular structures called **giant ionic lattices**.

Cl$^-$ion
Na$^+$ion

- There are strong forces of attraction between millions of oppositely charged ions.
- So ionic compounds have high melting points.

Ionic compounds don't conduct electricity when they are solid. However, they do if you melt them or dissolve them in water. The ions are then free to move around and carry the charge through the liquid. **D** **H**

solid

ions vibrate, but are fixed in position

off

melt   dissolve in water

on

ions free to move in molten compound   ions free to move in solution

Answers: 1 They vibrate. 2 They vibrate more vigorously (quickly). 3 Atoms are neutral, whereas ions are charged. 4 A substance made of two or more types of atom bonded together. 5 Na$^+$ and Cl$^-$ 6 2 electrons

12

▷ Covalent bonding

> Atoms of non-metals can bond to each other by **sharing pairs of electrons**.

This is **covalent bonding**.

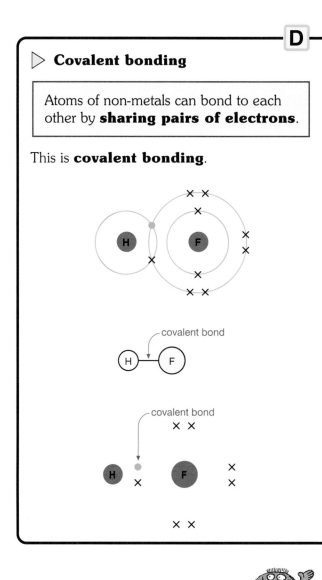

covalent bond

covalent bond

Take care:

Atoms that lose electrons form positive ions – they have more protons than electrons in their ions!

▷ Properties of covalent substances

Many covalently bonded substances are made up of small individual molecules (for example, water).

These have low melting points and boiling points because the forces **between** molecules are relatively weak.

Other substances with covalent bonds have **giant covalent structures**.

These have very high melting points (for example, diamond and graphite).

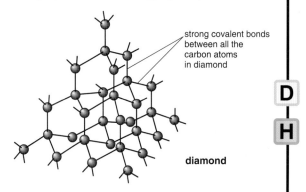

strong covalent bonds between all the carbon atoms in diamond

diamond

D

H

Graphite is the only non-metallic element that is a good conductor of electricity.

Look at the diagram below:

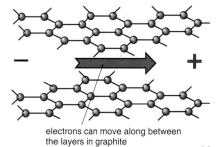

electrons can move along between the layers in graphite

graphite

D—**H**

▷ Metallic bonding

The atoms (or positive ions) in a metal are held to each other by a 'sea' of free electrons. These electrons:

- hold the atoms (or ions) together in giant structures,
- can drift though the metal when it conducts,
- let the atoms (or ions) slip over each other when hit or stretched.

metal atoms (some people describe them as **positive ions** because they donate electrons into the 'sea' of electrons)

'sea' of electrons holds the metal atoms (or ions) together

More in **Chemistry for You**, pages 262–86.

Examination Questions – Bonding

1 The diagram shows a model of part of the giant lattice of a metal.

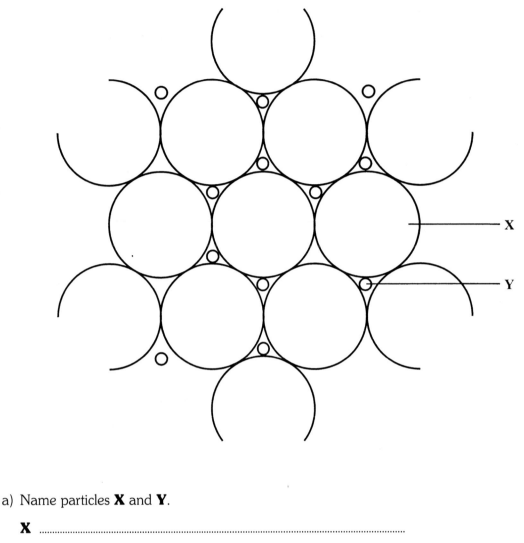

a) Name particles **X** and **Y**.

   X ....

   Y .... *(2 marks)*

b) Explain in terms of the giant structure above, why it is possible to bend a piece of metal.

   ....

   ....

   ....

   ....

   (2 marks)

c) Why can metals conduct electricity?

   ....

   ....

   ....

   (2 marks)   <u>6</u>

2 Magnesium burns in oxygen to form magnesium oxide.

a) Balance the equation for the reaction between magnesium and oxygen.

................Mg + O_2 ⟶ ....MgO

(1 mark)

b) Use pages 101 and 102 to help you answer these questions.

i The electronic structure of a magnesium atom can be represented as shown below.
Draw a similar diagram for an oxygen atom.

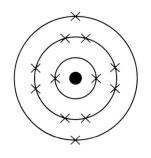

magnesium atom   oxygen atom   *(1 mark)*

ii The electronic structure of an oxide ion can be represented as shown below.
Draw a similar diagram to show the electronic structure of a magnesium ion.

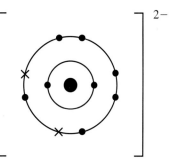

magnesium ion   oxide ion   *(2 marks)*

c) Magnesium oxide is used in making linings for furnaces.
Explain why ionic substances, such as magnesium oxide, have high melting points.

....

....

....

....

(2 marks)

d) The elements in Group 2, like the elements in Group 1, become more reactive lower down the Group.
Explain why.

....

....

....

....

(3 marks)   9

Getting the Grades – Classifying materials

Try this question, then compare your answer with the two examples opposite ▶

1   This question is about the particles which make up the atoms of all elements.

   a) The diagram below shows the arrangement of particles in an atom of carbon.

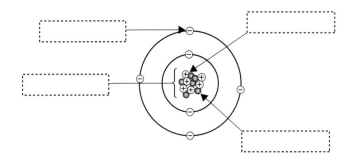

   The labels have been left off the diagram. Use words from the list to add labels to the diagram using the blank boxes provided.

   proton, nucleus, neutron, electron   (4 marks)

   b) It is not always necessary to use a diagram to describe an atom like this. A shorthand can be used instead. The carbon atom shown can be represented as follows:

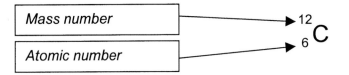

   What information is provided by:

   i   The atomic number .... (1 mark)

   ii The mass number .... (1 mark)

   c) Another isotope of carbon exists whose atoms have two more neutrons in them than the atom represented above.

   i   Use the shorthand to represent this atom in the space below:

                                                                                                          (2 marks)

   ii What do you understand by the term isotope?

   .... (1 mark)

   iii How will the electronic structure of these two isotopes of carbon compare with one another?

   .... (1 mark)

   d) Elements in the same column of the periodic table have similar chemical properties.
   The element below carbon in the periodic table is Silicon (atomic no. 14). Use ideas of atomic structure to help explain why these two elements have similar properties.

   ....

   .... (2 marks)

                                                                                            [Total 12 marks]

GRADE 'A' ANSWER

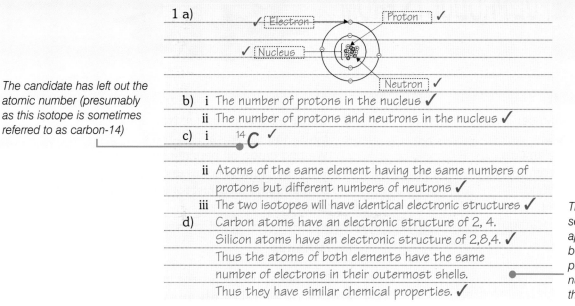

1 a)

✓ Electron   Proton ✓

✓ Nucleus

Neutron ✓

The candidate has left out the atomic number (presumably as this isotope is sometimes referred to as carbon-14)

b) i The number of protons in the nucleus ✓

ii The number of protons and neutrons in the nucleus ✓

c) i ^{14}C ✓

ii Atoms of the same element having the same numbers of protons but different numbers of neutrons ✓

iii The two isotopes will have identical electronic structures ✓

d) Carbon atoms have an electronic structure of 2, 4.
Silicon atoms have an electronic structure of 2,8,4. ✓
Thus the atoms of both elements have the same number of electrons in their outermost shells.
Thus they have similar chemical properties. ✓

The candidate gets the second mark for appreciating the link between chemical properties and the number of electrons in the outermost shell

11 marks = Grade A answer

▶ Improve your Grades   A up to A*

Use electronic structures to make more sense of the periodic table. Pay attention to the number of electrons in the outermost shell and also the number of shells. By knowing the period number (number of shells) and the group number (number of electrons in outermost shell) you will be able to make a number of predictions about the element under consideration. In particular the charge on the most common ion of the element can be predicted, or the number of covalent bonds which its atoms form.

GRADE 'C' ANSWER

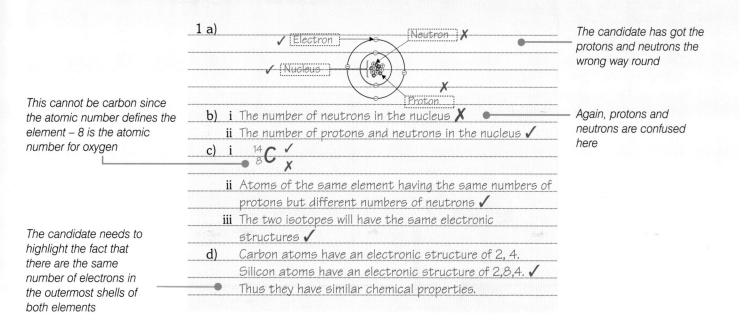

1 a)

✓ Electron   Neutron ✗

✓ Nucleus

✗

Proton

The candidate has got the protons and neutrons the wrong way round

This cannot be carbon since the atomic number defines the element – 8 is the atomic number for oxygen

b) i The number of neutrons in the nucleus ✗

ii The number of protons and neutrons in the nucleus ✓

c) i $^{14}_{8}C$ ✓ ✗

Again, protons and neutrons are confused here

ii Atoms of the same element having the same numbers of protons but different numbers of neutrons ✓

iii The two isotopes will have the same electronic structures ✓

d) Carbon atoms have an electronic structure of 2, 4.
Silicon atoms have an electronic structure of 2,8,4. ✓
Thus they have similar chemical properties.

The candidate needs to highlight the fact that there are the same number of electrons in the outermost shells of both elements

7 marks = Grade C answer

▶ Improve your Grades   C up to B

Mixing up protons and neutrons has cost marks in this answer. Remember: **P**rotons are **P**ositive and **N**eutrons are **N**eutral!
It is worth spending some time becoming familiar with the periodic table provided on page 102. It is worth remembering the two isotopes of carbon dealt with in this question, as well as the two isotopes of chlorine with mass numbers of 35 and 37.

3 USEFUL PRODUCTS FROM

⊳ **Crude oil**

Most of the compounds in crude oil are called **hydrocarbons**. They contain only hydrogen and carbon atoms.

Crude oil contains a **mixture of hydrocarbons**.

(A mixture consists of two or more elements or compounds that are **not** chemically combined. The substances in the mixture still have their original properties. This allows them to be separated.)

The hydrocarbons in crude oil all have different boiling points. They can be separated into compounds with similar boiling points by **fractional distillation**.

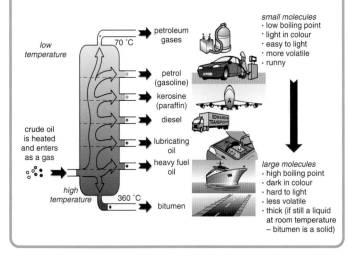

⊳ **Alkanes**

H

Many of the hydrocarbons in crude oil are called **alkanes**.

Their molecules contain only single bonds. They are known as **saturated** hydrocarbons.

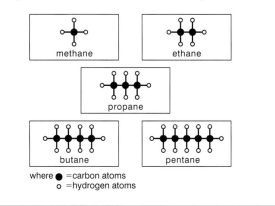

where ● = carbon atoms
○ = hydrogen atoms

⊳ **Cracking**

Most of the fractions from crude oil are used as fuels.
Fuels such as petrol are in great demand.
So some large hydrocarbon molecules in the heavier fractions are **'cracked'** into smaller, more useful molecules to use as fuels.
For example:

$$\text{decane} \longrightarrow \text{octane} + \text{ethene}$$
$$C_{10}H_{22} \longrightarrow C_8H_{18} + C_2H_4$$

The large molecules are heated and passed over a catalyst to break them down.
Cracking is an example of a **thermal decomposition** reaction.

▷ Polymers

During cracking, we also get small reactive molecules, such as ethene, formed.
These can react with each other when heated under pressure.

In the presence of a catalyst, these molecules join together to make large molecules used to make plastics.

> The small molecules are called **monomers**.
> The large molecule they form is called a **polymer**.
> The reaction is called **addition polymerisation.**

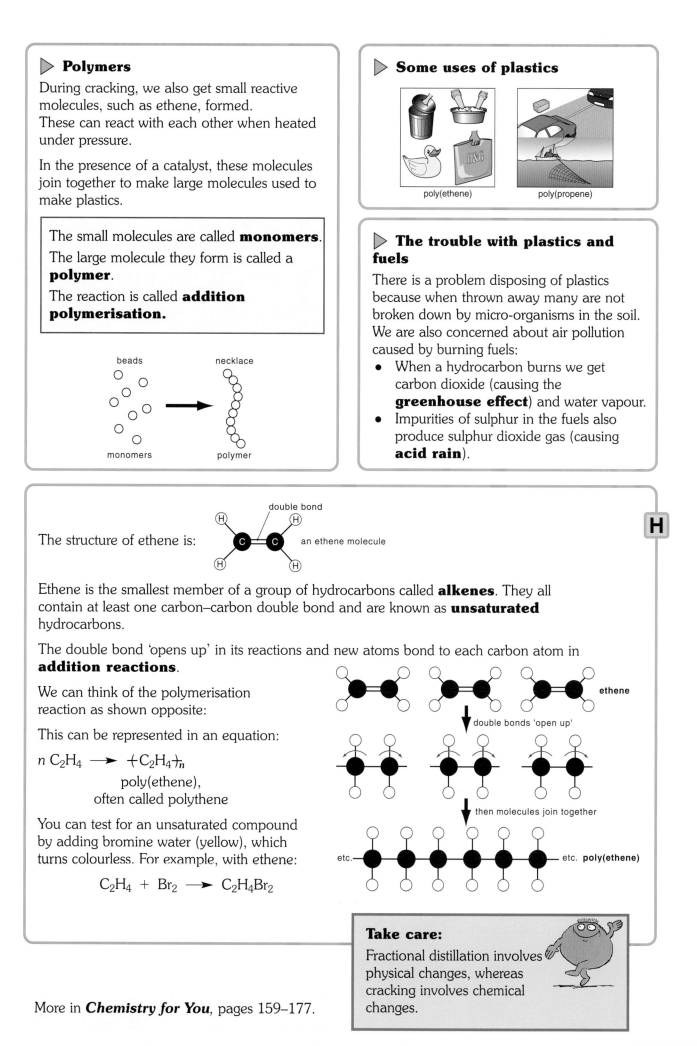

beads   necklace

monomers   polymer

▷ Some uses of plastics

poly(ethene)   poly(propene)

▷ The trouble with plastics and fuels

There is a problem disposing of plastics because when thrown away many are not broken down by micro-organisms in the soil. We are also concerned about air pollution caused by burning fuels:

- When a hydrocarbon burns we get carbon dioxide (causing the **greenhouse effect**) and water vapour.
- Impurities of sulphur in the fuels also produce sulphur dioxide gas (causing **acid rain**).

The structure of ethene is:

double bond

an ethene molecule

H

Ethene is the smallest member of a group of hydrocarbons called **alkenes**. They all contain at least one carbon–carbon double bond and are known as **unsaturated** hydrocarbons.

The double bond 'opens up' in its reactions and new atoms bond to each carbon atom in **addition reactions**.

We can think of the polymerisation reaction as shown opposite:

This can be represented in an equation:

$n \, C_2H_4 \longrightarrow \; +C_2H_4\,)_n$
      poly(ethene),
      often called polythene

You can test for an unsaturated compound by adding bromine water (yellow), which turns colourless. For example, with ethene:

$$C_2H_4 + Br_2 \longrightarrow C_2H_4Br_2$$

ethene

double bonds 'open up'

then molecules join together

etc.   etc. **poly(ethene)**

Take care:
Fractional distillation involves physical changes, whereas cracking involves chemical changes.

More in *Chemistry for You*, pages 159–177.

Examination Questions – Useful products from oil

Marks

1 a) Complete this sentence about crude oil.

   Crude oil is mainly a mixture of compounds called .... which
   contain carbon and hydrogen only.   *(1 mark)*

   b) The diagram shows a laboratory experiment used to separate crude oil.

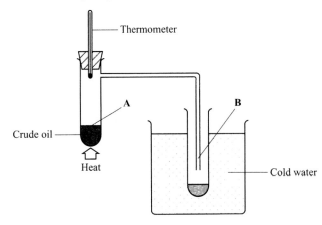

   Complete each sentence by choosing the correct words from the box.

condensation	distillation	evaporation	melting	sublimation

   The main process taking place at **A** is ....

   The main process taking place at **B** is ....

   This method of separating crude oil is called ....

                                                                        (3 marks)

   c) Complete this sentence by crossing out the word in each box that is wrong. The first one
   has been done for you.

   This method of separating crude oil works because the   smaller ~~larger~~   the molecules

   are, the   higher / lower   their boiling point and the   more / less   volatile they are.   *(1 mark)*

   d) Poly(ethene) is a plastic made from crude oil. It is a useful plastic but it can cause
   problems because it is **not** biodegradable.

   i   Give **one** use of poly(ethene).

   ....   *(1 mark)*

   ii Explain the meaning of biodegradable.

   ....

   ....   *(1 mark)*

   iii Suggest reasons why the disposal of poly(ethene) may cause environmental problems.

   ....

   ....

   ....

   ....   *(2 marks)*   9

2 The many hydrocarbons in crude oil are separated into fractions.

a) Some of the larger hydrocarbon molecules can be broken down to produce smaller, more useful hydrocarbon molecules.

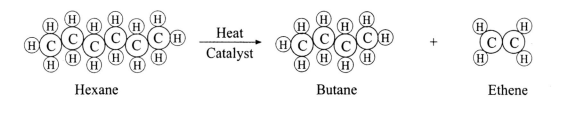

Hexane   Butane   Ethene

Hexane and butane are alkanes. Describe the structure of alkanes.

....

....

....

....

....

....

....

(3 marks)

b) Ethene is used to make poly(ethene).

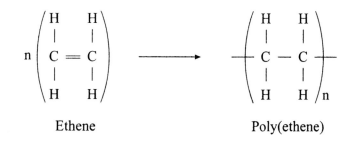

Ethene   Poly(ethene)

This process is called polymerisation. Explain what is meant by polymerisation.

....

....

....

....

....

(2 marks)

5

4 Useful products from METAL ORES

▶ ThinkAbout:

1 Name a metal that is less reactive than copper.
2 Which metal is used to make cooking foil?
3 Which metal is used to make electrical wires in household appliances?

4 Why are iron gates usually painted?
5 What do we call it when a compound is broken down by electricity?

▶ The Reactivity Series

Metals can be put into order of reactivity in the **Reactivity Series**.

The metals higher up the Reactivity Series can **displace** those lower down from their compounds. For example:

magnesium + copper sulphate ⟶ magnesium sulphate + copper
Mg + $CuSO_4$ ⟶ $MgSO_4$ + Cu

Metals are found in the Earth's crust as metals themselves (for example, gold) or as metal compounds.

> **Ores** are rocks that contain enough metal or its compound to make it economic to extract the metal.

We can predict how to extract a metal from its position in the Reactivity Series.

The highly reactive metals are difficult to extract.

We use electrolysis to extract these metals, such as sodium or aluminium.
The metals of medium reactivity can be extracted by reduction of the oxides with carbon.

potassium
sodium
magnesium
aluminium
CARBON
zinc
iron
tin
lead
copper

carbon cannot be used to extract the more reactive metals

- - - - - - - - -

these metals can be extracted using carbon

▶ The blast furnace

We extract iron in a giant **blast furnace**.

1. The coke (carbon) reacts with oxygen in the hot air to make carbon dioxide.
   $C(s) + O_2(g) \longrightarrow CO_2(g)$

2. This carbon dioxide reacts with more hot coke to make **carbon monoxide** gas.
   $CO_2(g) + C(s) \longrightarrow 2\,CO(g)$

3. The carbon monoxide then **reduces** the iron oxide to iron.
   $Fe_2O_3(s) + 3\,CO(g) \longrightarrow 2\,Fe(l) + 3\,CO_2(g)$

4. Limestone gets rid of the sandy bits (acidic impurities) in the iron ore. They form a liquid **slag**.

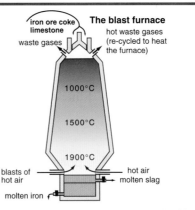

The blast furnace

iron ore coke limestone
waste gases
hot waste gases (re-cycled to heat the furnace)
1000°C
1500°C
1900°C
blasts of hot air
hot air
molten slag
molten iron

The iron from a blast furnace goes on to make **steel** (which usually contains over 95% iron). We have to protect the iron in steel from rusting. We can stop air and water getting to the iron by forming a barrier, for example by coating it with paint, plastic or tin.

However, it is more effective to attach a more reactive metal than iron (such as zinc or magnesium). The more reactive metal reacts in preference to iron and so protects it from rusting. This is called **sacrificial protection**. We can also add a little nickel or chromium in the steel-making process to form stainless steel (used for cutlery).

▶ **Electrolysis** is the breakdown of a substance by electricity.

It is used to extract reactive metals, such as **aluminium**. Aluminium is found in its ore **bauxite**, which contains aluminium oxide.
The aluminium oxide is dissolved in molten cryolite. This lowers the melting point of aluminium oxide.

an aluminium plant uses the same amount of electricity as a small town

the lining of the cell is a carbon cathode

molten aluminium

carbon anodes

molten aluminium oxide (dissolved in molten cryolite)

molten aluminium is tapped or syphoned off from the cell

The electrodes are made of carbon.
Aluminium forms at the **cathode (−)**.
Carbon dioxide is given off from the **anode (+)**.
(The oxygen from the aluminium oxide reacts with the carbon anode to make carbon dioxide, so the anode gets burned away and has to be replaced frequently.)

The aluminium made is a very useful metal.
It resists corrosion because it is covered in a tough layer of aluminium oxide.
We can make it stronger by forming **alloys** by mixing in small amounts of other metals, such as magnesium.
These alloys are much harder and stiffer than pure aluminium.

▶ **Copper** is **purified** by electrolysis.
The anode is the impure copper. The cathode is pure copper.

The copper electrodes dip into a solution containing copper ions which are positively charged.

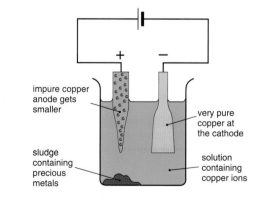

impure copper anode gets smaller

sludge containing precious metals

very pure copper at the cathode

solution containing copper ions

More in *Chemistry for You*, pages 79–117.

During electrolysis, reactions at the negative electrode (cathode) are called reduction:

e.g. $Al^{3+} + 3e^- \longrightarrow Al$
$Cu^{2+} + 2e^- \longrightarrow Cu$

Reduction is the gain of electrons.

Whilst at the positive electrode (anode), oxidation takes place:

e.g. $2O^{2-} \longrightarrow O_2 + 4e^-$
$Cu \longrightarrow Cu^{2+} + 2e^-$

Oxidation is the loss of electrons.

In chemical reactions, if one substance is reduced another is always oxidised; so the reactions are called **redox** reactions.

Examination Questions – Useful products from metal ores

(You will need to have covered Topic 9 to answer questions 1 and 3.)

1 Iron is the most commonly used metal. Iron is extracted in a blast furnace form iron oxide using carbon monoxide.

$$Fe_2O_3 + 3CO \longrightarrow 2Fe + 3CO_2$$

a) A sample of the ore haematite contains 70% iron oxide.
   Calculate the amount of iron oxide in 2000 tonnes of haematite.

   ....

   ....

   Amount of iron oxide = ... tonnes

   (1 mark)

b) Calculate the amount of iron that can be extracted from 2000 tonnes of haematite.

   (Relative atomic masses: O = 16; Fe = 56)

   ....

   ....

   ....

   ....

   ....

   Amount of iron = ... tonnes

   (3 marks)   4

2 Aluminium oxide (Al_2O_3) is an ionic compound. It has a very high melting point.

   a) Explain why ionic compounds have high melting points.

   ....

   ....

   ....

   (1 mark)

   b) The diagram shows the atoms that form aluminium oxide.

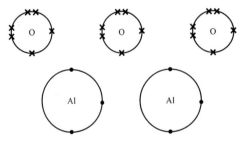

   On the diagram, show the movements of electrons that occur to form aluminium oxide from these atoms.   *(3 marks)*

   c) Aluminium is manufactured by the electrolysis of molten aluminium oxide.
      Balance the half equation for the reaction at the negative electrode.

   $$Al^{3+} + e^- \longrightarrow Al$$ *(1 mark)*   5

3   a) The diagram shows a blast furnace used to extract iron from iron ore.

Complete the diagram by adding the **three** missing labels.

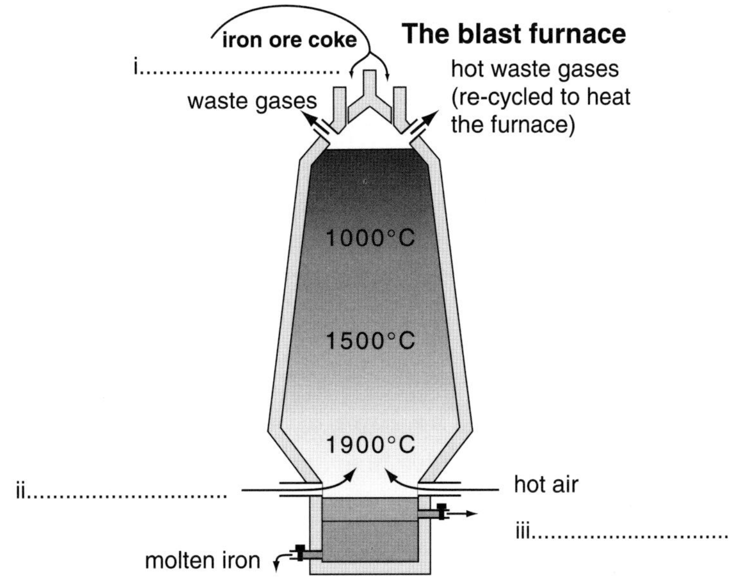

The blast furnace

iron ore coke

i.............................

waste gases

hot waste gases
(re-cycled to heat
the furnace)

1000°C

1500°C

1900°C

ii.............................

hot air

iii.............................

molten iron

(3 marks)

b) An important reaction in this process is represented by this equation.

i Balance the equation.

$$Fe_2O_3 + 3CO \longrightarrow \text{..........} Fe + \text{..........} CO_2$$

(1 mark)

ii Which substance has been reduced in this reaction?

.... *(1 mark)*

c) Iron ore contains iron oxide.

i Calculate the relative formula mass of iron oxide, Fe_2O_3.

(Relative atomic masses: = 16; Fe = 56)

....

....

Answer = ...

(2 marks)

ii Calculate the percentage by mass of iron in iron oxide.

....

Percentage of iron = ... %

(2 marks)

iii Calculate the mass of iron that could be extracted from 1000 kg of iron oxide. Use your answer to part c) ii to help you with this calculation.

....

Mass of iron = ... kg

(1 mark)

10

25

5 Useful products from rocks and air

> ## ThinkAbout:

1. Name three rocks that are made mainly from calcium carbonate.
2. What do we call the reaction between an acid and an alkali?
3. Which gas makes up most of the air?
4. What is the reactive gas in the air?

FROM ROCKS

> ### Limestone

Limestone is made up mainly of **calcium carbonate** ($CaCO_3$). It is used as a building material itself, but is also used to make **cement**.

Powdered limestone is heated in a rotating kiln with clay (or shale) to make the cement.

Cement is the basis of **concrete** – the most widely used building material. This is made by mixing cement, sand and crushed rock, together with water. The mixture sets in a slow chemical reaction to form a very hard, rock-like substance.

D

> ### Glass

We make glass by heating sand, limestone and soda (sodium carbonate).

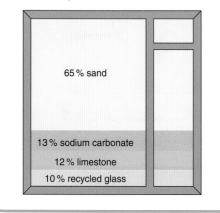

- 65 % sand
- 13 % sodium carbonate
- 12 % limestone
- 10 % recycled glass

> ### The lime kiln

When we heat limestone in a lime kiln it makes quicklime (calcium oxide, CaO), also known as lime:

$$CaCO_3(s) \longrightarrow CaO(s) + CO_2(g)$$

The reaction is called **thermal decomposition**.

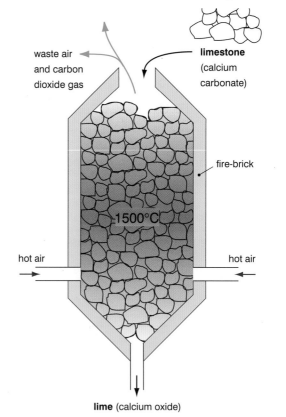

waste air and carbon dioxide gas

limestone (calcium carbonate)

fire-brick

1500°C

hot air

hot air

lime (calcium oxide)

By adding water to quicklime, we get slaked lime (calcium hydroxide, $Ca(OH)_2$) which is a cheap alkali. This, or powdered limestone, can be used to raise the pH of acidic soil.

Powdered limestone is also used to neutralise lakes affected by acid rain.

Answers: 1 limestone, chalk and marble   2 neutralisation   3 nitrogen   4 oxygen

FROM AIR

▷ Making ammonia – the Haber process

Although almost 80% of the air is nitrogen gas, most plants can't use this directly to help them grow. So we add nitrogen-based **fertilisers** to the soil.

These are soluble compounds that can be absorbed through the roots of a plant.

However, these fertilisers do cause pollution in our water supplies and in rivers.

Nitrogen is converted to ammonia (NH_3) in the **Haber process**:

$$\text{nitrogen} + \text{hydrogen} \rightleftharpoons \text{ammonia}$$
$$N_2(g) + 3H_2(g) \rightleftharpoons 2NH_3(g)$$

- The catalyst used is iron.
- The temperature is about 450 °C.
- The pressure is about 200 atmospheres.

> **Facts about the Haber process**
>
> **Raw materials**
> Air (for nitrogen)
> Natural gas (to make hydrogen)
> Steam (to make hydrogen and to generate high pressures)
>
> **Conditions**
> Temperature : about 450 °C
> Pressure : about 200 atmospheres
> Catalyst : mainly iron

These conditions are chosen to give a reasonable yield of ammonia as quickly as possible.
The ammonia gas is cooled down. It condenses to a liquid that is collected.
Any unreacted nitrogen and hydrogen are recycled to the start of the process.

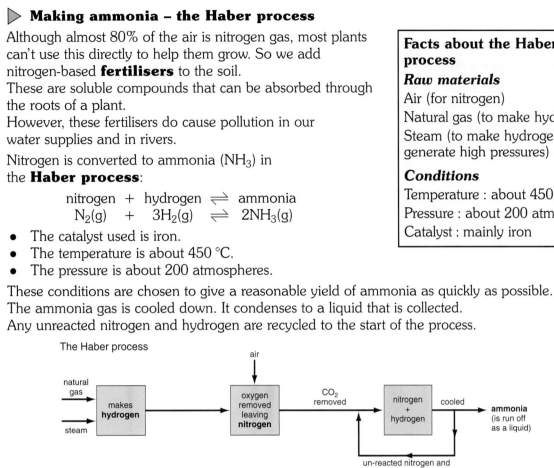

The Haber process

▷ Making nitric acid and ammonium nitrate fertiliser

Some of the ammonia is used to make **nitric acid** (HNO_3).
Ammonia is oxidised to nitrogen monoxide and water by passing it over a hot platinum catalyst:

$$\text{ammonia} + \text{oxygen} \rightleftharpoons \text{nitrogen monoxide} + \text{water}$$

This nitrogen monoxide is then cooled down and reacted with more oxygen and water to make the nitric acid:

$$\text{nitrogen monoxide} + \text{oxygen} \rightleftharpoons \text{nitrogen dioxide}$$
$$\text{nitrogen dioxide} + \text{oxygen} + \text{water} \longrightarrow \text{nitric acid}$$

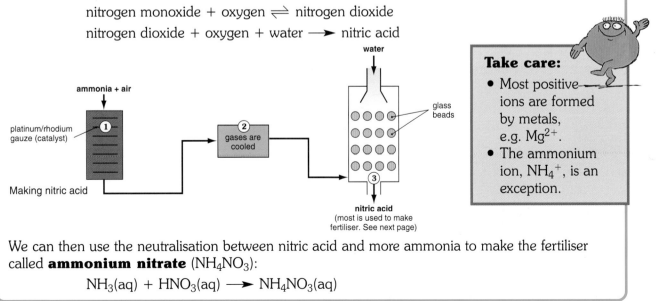

Making nitric acid

> **Take care:**
> - Most positive ions are formed by metals, e.g. Mg^{2+}.
> - The ammonium ion, NH_4^+, is an exception.

We can then use the neutralisation between nitric acid and more ammonia to make the fertiliser called **ammonium nitrate** (NH_4NO_3):

$$NH_3(aq) + HNO_3(aq) \longrightarrow NH_4NO_3(aq)$$

More in *Chemistry for You*, pages 127–134 and 242–251.

Examination Questions – Useful products from rocks and air

1 The diagram shows the final stages in the manufacture of ammonia.

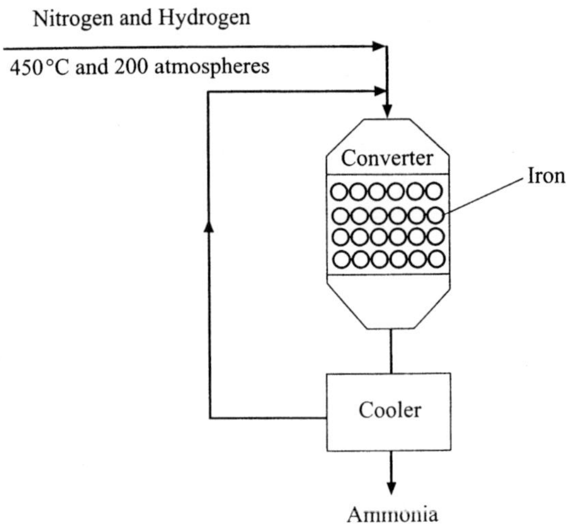

Nitrogen and Hydrogen

450 °C and 200 atmospheres

Converter

Iron

Cooler

Ammonia

a) Why is iron used in the converter?

....

.... *(1 mark)*

b) Write the word equation for the reaction in the converter.

.... + ... $\rightleftharpoons$ .... *(1 mark)*

c) The yield of ammonia is only about 15%.

i Why can the yield not be 100%.

....

.... *(1 mark)*

ii Describe what happens to the mixture of gases after it leaves the converter.

....

.... *(2 marks)*

5

2 Nitric acid is made from ammonia, NH_3.

The first stage in this process can be shown in a flow diagram.

Look at the flow diagram opposite.

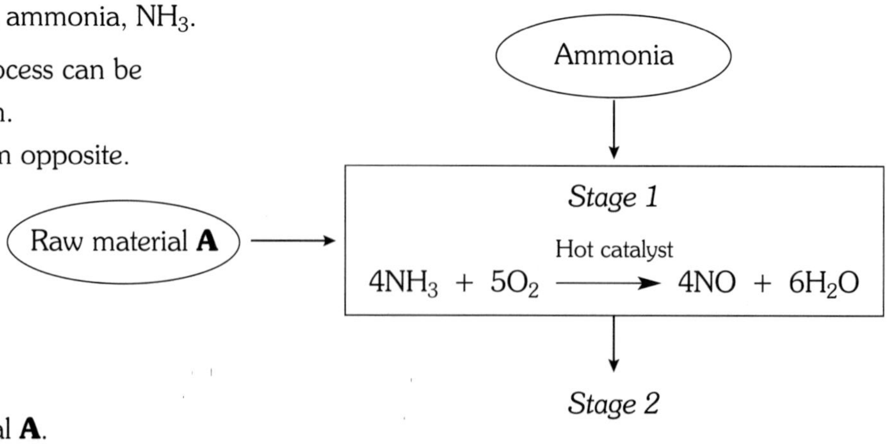

Ammonia

Raw material **A**

Stage 1

Hot catalyst

$4NH_3 + 5O_2 \longrightarrow 4NO + 6H_2O$

Stage 2

a) Name raw material **A**.

.... *(1 mark)*

b) Draw a ring around:

i the name of the catalyst used in stage 1;

gold   iron   mercury   platinum   *(1 mark)*

ii the word which best describes this reaction.

decomposition   displacement   neutralisation   oxidation (*1 mark*)

c) Nitric acid can be neutralised by alkalis to make salts.

i The salt called potassium nitrate can be made from nitric acid.
Complete the word equation for this neutralisation reaction.
Choose the correct substances from the box.

> **hydrogen   oxygen   potassium chloride**
>
> **potassium hydroxide   water**

nitric acid + ... ⟶ potassium nitrate + ...

(*2 marks*)

ii Ammonium nitrate is another salt made from nitric acid.

Which **one** of the following is the main use of ammonium nitrate?
Draw a ring around your answer.

dye   fertiliser   plastic   fuel (*1 mark*)

iii Complete this sentence by choosing the correct ion from the box.

> H^+ NH_4^+ NO_3^- O^{2-} OH^-

The ion that makes solutions acidic is .... (*1 mark*)   7

3 This question is about the use of limestone in industry. The diagram shows a kiln which is used to convert limestone into lime (quicklime).

a) Complete the diagram by adding the chemical names of the substances into the spaces given.   (*3 marks*)

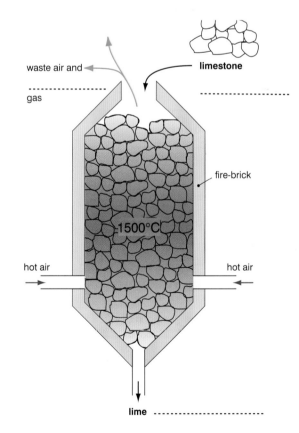

waste air and
gas

limestone

fire-brick

1500°C

hot air   hot air

lime

b) In this reaction heating causes the limestone to break down into two simpler substances.
What is the name used to describe this type of reaction ?

.... (*2 marks*)   5

6 Representing reactions

▷ **ThinkAbout:**

1 Hydrogen chloride gas is formed when hydrogen burns in chlorine gas.
Write a word equation for this reaction.

2 Write a balanced equation, including state symbols, for the reaction described in question 1.
(Chemical formulae needed: hydrogen = H_2, chlorine = Cl_2, hydrogen chloride = HCl)

▷ **Conservation of mass**

We can classify changes as physical changes or chemical changes:

- **Physical changes** do not produce any new substances, and are often easy to reverse. Changes of state, such as melting or boiling, are examples of physical changes.

- However, in **chemical changes** (or reactions) new substances are made. There are energy changes that accompany chemical changes. Burning carbon is an example of a chemical change.

We can represent these chemical reactions by **word equations**:

reactants ⟶ products

For example:

carbon + oxygen ⟶ carbon dioxide

The law of **conservation of mass** states that:

the total mass of the reactants **equals** the total mass of the products.

▲

▷ **Balanced equations**

Chemical reactions can also be shown by **balanced equations** made up of chemical formulae. These must have the same numbers of each type of atom on either side of the equation. For example:

$$2H_2 + O_2 \longrightarrow 2H_2O$$

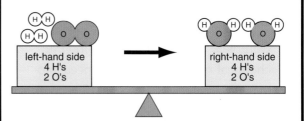

left-hand side
4 H's
2 O's

right-hand side
4 H's
2 O's

We can also include state symbols (s), (l), (g) or (aq).

Where:

s = solid

l = liquid

g = gas

aq = aqueous (dissolved in water)

For example:

$$2Na(s) + 2H_2O(l) \longrightarrow 2NaOH(aq) + H_2(g)$$

Answers: 1 hydrogen + chlorine ⟶ hydrogen chloride 2 $H_2(g) + Cl_2(g) \longrightarrow 2HCl(g)$

▷ Half equations in electrolysis

We can also write half equations to describe the reactions at each electrode during electrolysis. For example, during the electrolysis of molten copper chloride or copper chloride solution:

At the **cathode** (negative electrode) we get:
$$Cu^{2+} + 2e^- \longrightarrow Cu$$

At the **anode** (positive electrode) we get:
$$2Cl^- - 2e^- \longrightarrow Cl_2$$

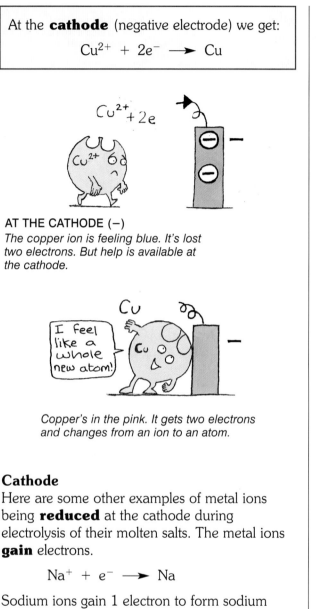

AT THE CATHODE (−)
The copper ion is feeling blue. It's lost two electrons. But help is available at the cathode.

Copper's in the pink. It gets two electrons and changes from an ion to an atom.

Cathode

Here are some other examples of metal ions being **reduced** at the cathode during electrolysis of their molten salts. The metal ions **gain** electrons.

$$Na^+ + e^- \longrightarrow Na$$

Sodium ions gain 1 electron to form sodium atoms.

$$Al^{3+} + 3e^- \longrightarrow Al$$

Aluminium ions each gain 3 electrons to form aluminium atoms.

More examples throughout **Chemistry for You**, especially pages 22–6, 105 and 115.

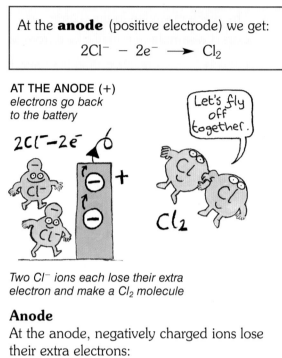

AT THE ANODE (+)
electrons go back to the battery

Let's fly off together.

Two Cl⁻ ions each lose their extra electron and make a Cl₂ molecule

Anode

At the anode, negatively charged ions lose their extra electrons:

$$2O^{2-} - 4e^- \longrightarrow O_2$$

The negatively charged ions are **oxidised** at the anode.

Take care:
- Positive metal ions have to *gain* electrons at the cathode in order to change into metal atoms.
- At the anode, *molecules* of gas often form, such as O_2 or Cl_2, not atoms.

Oxidation
Is
Loss of electrons

Reduction
Is
Gain of electrons

Examination Questions – Representing reactions

1 Smelting with Carbon

This question is about extracting metals from their compounds using the element carbon.

a) The reaction shown in the diagram can be used to extract a sample of metallic lead from lead oxide.

Carbon is more reactive than lead and therefore combines with the oxygen in the lead oxide. The carbon dioxide formed is given off leaving the lead behind.

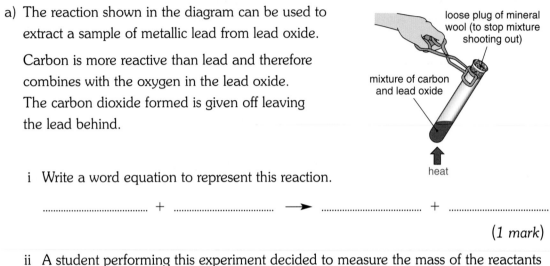

loose plug of mineral wool (to stop mixture shooting out)

mixture of carbon and lead oxide

heat

 i Write a word equation to represent this reaction.

.... + ... $\longrightarrow$ .... + ...

(1 mark)

 ii A student performing this experiment decided to measure the mass of the reactants and products obtained. The results are shown below. One result is missing – use the three values given to work out what the fourth value should be.

Substance	mass/g
Lead oxide	446
Carbon	12

Substance	mass/g
Lead	414
Carbon dioxide	....

(1 mark)

b) A number of similar reactions are used in a blast furnace to extract iron from its ore.

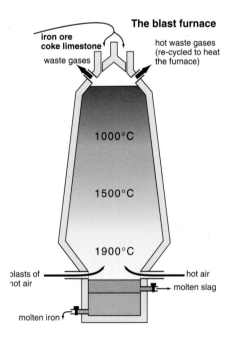

The blast furnace

iron ore
coke limestone
waste gases

hot waste gases (re-cycled to heat the furnace)

1000°C

1500°C

1900°C

blasts of hot air

hot air

molten slag

molten iron

The reactions taking place in the blast furnace can be described as follows:

1. Carbon combines with oxygen to form carbon dioxide.

2. Carbon dioxide combines with carbon to form carbon monoxide.

3. Iron oxide is reduced by carbon monoxide to give iron and carbon dioxide.

i Write a word equation for reaction 2.

Marks

.... + ... $\longrightarrow$ ....

(1 mark)

ii The word equation for reaction 1 can be written as

carbon + oxygen $\longrightarrow$ carbon dioxide

Give the symbol equation for this reaction (including state symbols).

.... + ... $\longrightarrow$ ....

(2 marks)

iii A symbol equation for the main reduction reaction can be shown as follows:

$Fe_2O_3(s)$ + ... $CO(g)$ $\longrightarrow$ .... $Fe(l)$ + ... $CO_2(g)$

The equation is not balanced. Add numbers in front of the symbols above to balance the equation.

(2 marks)   7

2 Extraction by electrolysis

This question is about using an electric current to obtain a sample of metal from one of its compounds.

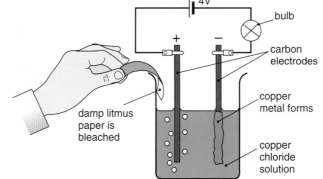

a) The electric current splits the copper chloride into its two constituent elements.

i Write a word equation to represent this reaction.

.... $\longrightarrow$ .... + ...

(1 mark)

ii A word equation for the reaction at the cathode, by which copper metal forms, is given below:

copper ions + electrons $\longrightarrow$ copper atoms

Write a balanced symbol equation for this change.

.... + ... $\longrightarrow$ ....

(2 marks)

iii A symbol equation for the reaction taking place at the anode can be written as follows:

.... $Cl^-(aq)$ $\longrightarrow$ .... $Cl_2(g)$ + ... e^-

Add numbers, where necessary, to the spaces in the equation in order to balance it.

(2 marks)   5

> **ThinkAbout:**

1 Name the main noble gas found in the air.
2 Why are people worried about increasing levels of carbon dioxide in the atmosphere?

3 What is the formula of:
a) oxygen gas b) nitrogen gas
c) argon gas?

D

> **The atmosphere**

The air is made up of about:
- 80% nitrogen gas
- 20% oxygen gas
- small amounts of other gases, including carbon dioxide, water vapour and noble gases.

History of the atmosphere

In the Earth's first billion years, its early atmosphere came from volcanoes.

It was probably mainly **carbon dioxide** (like Mars and Venus now). There was no oxygen. This only arrived once the first plants had evolved.

During photosynthesis, the plants took in carbon dioxide and gave out oxygen.

Most carbon became 'trapped' in fossil fuels and carbonate rocks. The oceans were formed when water vapour from the volcanoes fell as rain as the Earth cooled down.

The small amount of ammonia and methane in the early atmosphere was removed when they reacted with oxygen gas.

The history of our atmosphere

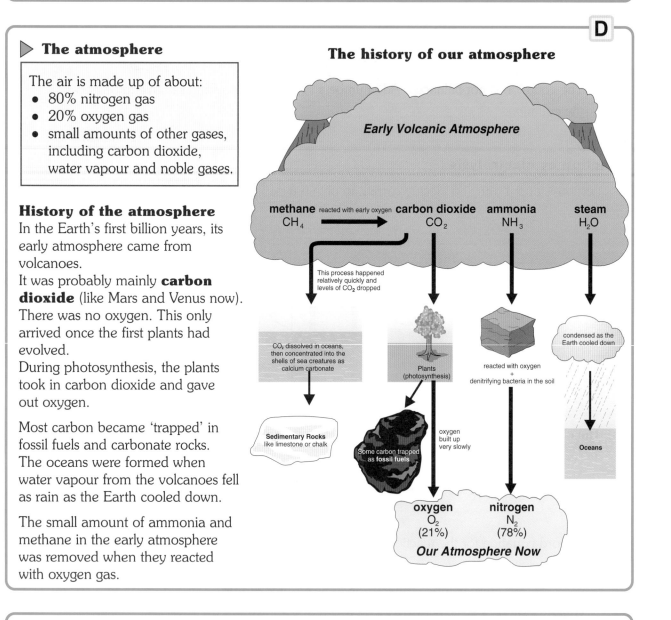

Most nitrogen in the atmosphere came from the action of **denitrifying bacteria** in the soil.

Some of the oxygen gas (O_2) in the air was converted to ozone gas (O_3). This formed the **ozone layer** in the upper atmosphere. This was an important stage in life developing on land.

D

H

The **ozone layer** protects the surface of the Earth from harmful ultraviolet radiation arriving from the Sun.

Answers: **1** argon **2** global warming/greenhouse effect **3** a) O_2 b) N_2 c) Ar

▷ The carbon cycle

The natural balance of carbon dioxide in the atmosphere is maintained in the carbon cycle:

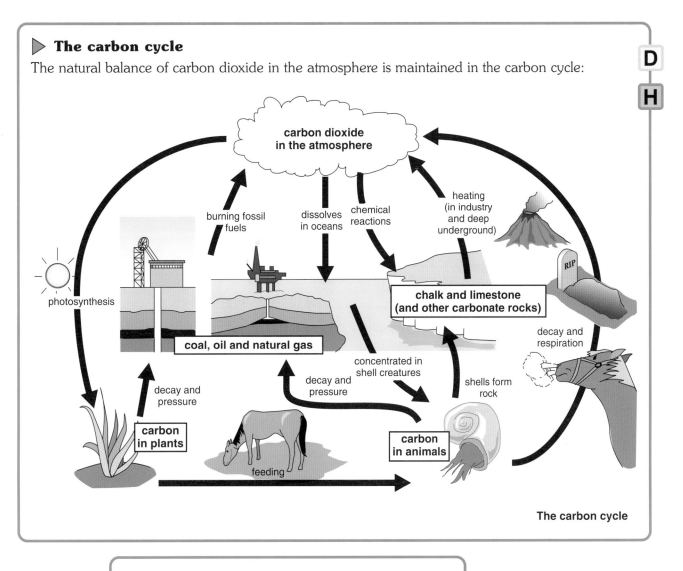

The carbon cycle

- The oceans act as a huge reservoir for carbon dioxide.
- The CO_2 gas reacts in the seawater to produce insoluble carbonates (which precipitate out as solids, such as calcium carbonate) and soluble hydrogencarbonates (such as those of calcium and magnesium).
- However, our burning of fossil fuels releases vast amounts of carbon dioxide into the atmosphere.
- As industrialisation increases, the oceans can no longer cope with the volumes of carbon dioxide (a 'greenhouse gas') produced.
- Most people are getting more and more concerned about the threat of global warming.

More in **Chemistry for You**,
pages 314–21.

Take care:

The timescales involved in the history of the atmosphere are vast – the current proportions of gases have been roughly constant for the last 200 million years!

Examination Questions – Changes to the Earth and atmosphere

1 The bar chart shows the percentage composition of the atmosphere on Mars.

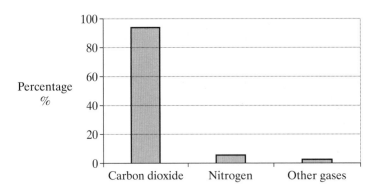

a) State three ways in which the atmosphere on Earth today is different from that on Mars.   Marks

1 ....

....

2 ....

....

3 ....

....

(3 marks)

b) The atmosphere on Earth may once have been like that on Mars. The evolution of green plants has changed the atmosphere on Earth.
Explain why.

....

....

....

(2 marks)   5

2 The graph on page 37 shows the amount of carbon dioxide in the atmosphere over the last 300 years.

a) Describe how the amount of carbon dioxide in the atmosphere has changed over the last 300 years.

....

.... (2 marks)

b) Use the words from the list to complete the sentences.

burning   distillation   electricity   fuels   pressure   temperature

The change in the amount of carbon dioxide in the atmosphere is caused partly by the

.... of .... One effect of this change in the amount

of carbon dioxide is the increase in the .... of the atmosphere.

(3 marks)   5

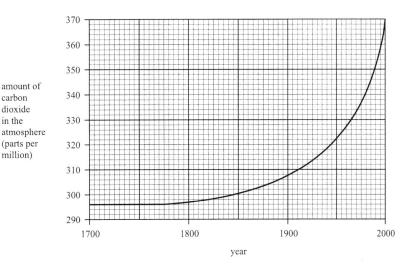

3 This question is about the way in which the Earth's atmosphere has changed since the Earth was formed. The table gives the composition of the atmosphere today.

The Earth's atmosphere

Gases in air	% of air	
nitrogen	78	
oxygen	21	
carbon dioxide	0.04	
water vapour	varies	1
argon	0.93	
other noble gases		

a) Use the words from the list below to complete the following passage:

photosynthesis, bacteria, oxygen, unreactive, decompose, nitrogen

The modern atmosphere is composed mainly of .... which is a very

... gas. This was produced partly as a result of the action of

... in the soil which .... nitrates in the soil. The

reactive gas .... which is essential for life was produced as a result of

... by green plants. (3 marks)

b) Scientists think that when the Earth was very young its atmosphere was made up mainly of carbon dioxide.

i What has happened to the carbon dioxide content of the atmosphere since the Earth was formed?

.... (1 mark)

ii What processes have helped to change the carbon dioxide content in this way?

....

.... (2 marks)

c) The atmosphere is constantly changing as a result of activity on the planet.
250 years ago the percentage of carbon dioxide in the atmosphere was 0.028%.

i How can we explain the change in the carbon dioxide content of the atmosphere over the last 250 years?

....

.... (2 marks)

ii This change is causing concern amongst many scientists. Why are they concerned?

....

.... (2 marks)

10

8 The rock record

▷ **ThinkAbout:**

1 These are examples of sedimentary rock:

c _ _ _ _   s _ _ _ _ _ _ _

m _ _ _ _ _ _ _   l _ _ _ _ _ _ _ _

c _ _ _ _ _ _ _ _ _ _ _

2 These are examples of metamorphic rock:

m _ _ _ _ _   s _ _ _ _

3 These are examples of igneous rock:

g _ _ _ _ _ _   b _ _ _ _ _

▷ **The rock cycle**

There are three main types of rock:

- **sedimentary**
- **metamorphic**
- **igneous.**

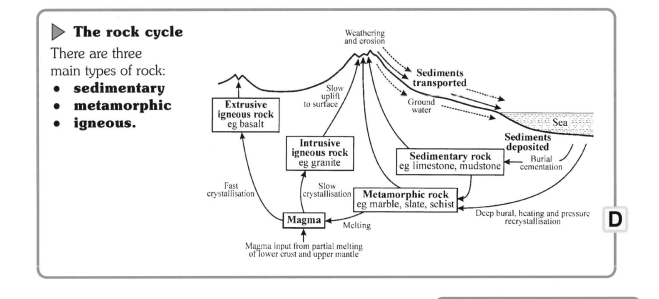

D

D

▷ **Sedimentary rocks**

> **Sedimentary rocks** are formed when bits of rock, shell or plants settle in layers.

As the layers build up the pressure increases. This fuses the edges of sediments together, and water in between sediments gets squeezed out. This leaves behind any solids dissolved in the water and the bits are, in effect, 'cemented' together.

The rock contains evidence of how the sediment was originally deposited, for example:

- Ripple marks show the direction of currents or waves.
- Sharp boundaries between neighbouring sedimentary layers indicate distinct periods when different sediments were laid down.

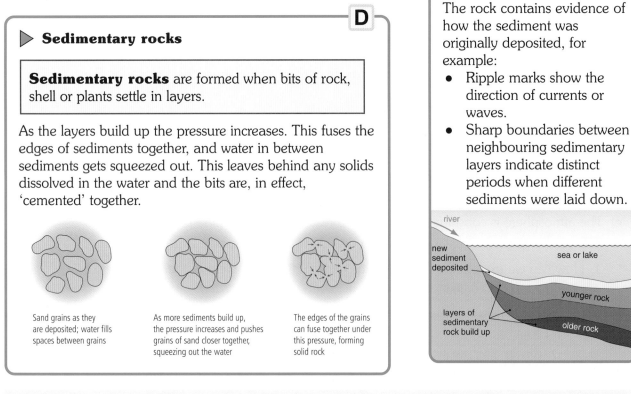

Sand grains as they are deposited; water fills spaces between grains

As more sediments build up, the pressure increases and pushes grains of sand closer together, squeezing out the water

The edges of the grains can fuse together under this pressure, forming solid rock

---

Answers: **1** chalk, sandstone, limestone, mudstone, conglomerate   **2** marble, slate   **3** granite, basalt

▷ Distorted layers

The layers of sedimentary rock are often found tilted, folded or fractured (faulted) by stress forces set up within the Earth's crust.

Occasionally the layers can even be turned upside down. In this case the younger rock will lie beneath the older layers.

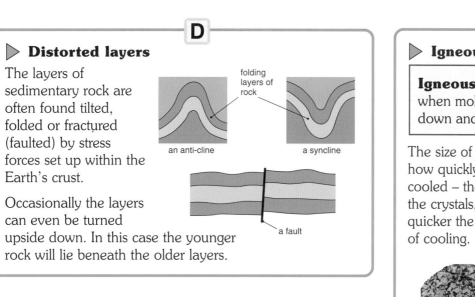

folding layers of rock

an anti-cline

a syncline

a fault

▷ Igneous rocks

Igneous rocks are made when molten rock cools down and forms crystals.

The size of the crystals tells us how quickly the molten rock cooled – the smaller the crystals, the quicker the rate of cooling.

▷ Metamorphic rocks

Metamorphic rocks are formed when rocks are put under great pressure and/or are heated to high temperatures (without melting).

Where the Earth's plates collide, mountains are built (replacing those worn away over millions of years by weathering and erosion).

You find metamorphic rocks in these mountain ranges. This is due to the great pressure and high temperatures produced as mountains form.

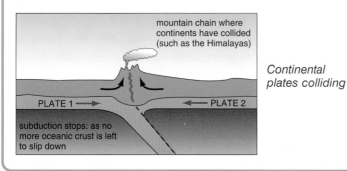

mountain chain where continents have collided (such as the Himalayas)

PLATE 1 →   ← PLATE 2

subduction stops: as no more oceanic crust is left to slip down

Continental plates colliding

Take care:
- Metamorphic rock formed under *pressure* will often have bands of minerals running through the rock. However those formed by *heating*, such as marble from limestone, will not have bands.
- The crystals in metamorphic rocks are difficult to see because they are usually very small.

More in ***Chemistry for You***, pages 323–46.

▷ Structure of the Earth

The Earth is made up from:
- a thin outer **crust**
- a **mantle** (under the crust stretching almost half-way to the centre of the Earth)
- a **core** (the outer core is liquid; the inner core is solid; both parts are made from iron and nickel).

The Earth's crust and uppermost part of its mantle (called the **lithosphere**) is split up into **tectonic plates**. These move very slowly on convection currents set up in the mantle. The heat comes from radioactive rocks.

We can work out the plate boundaries by looking at where we get earthquakes and volcanoes.

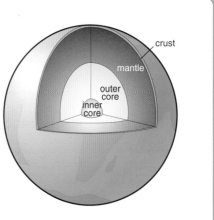

crust

mantle

outer core

inner core

Examination Questions – The rock record

1 a) The diagram shows the layered structure of the Earth.

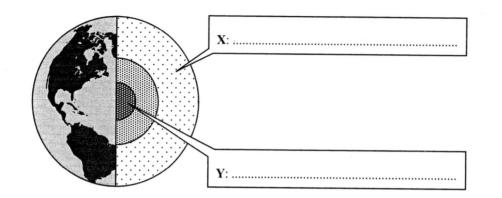

X: ....

Y: ....

    i Write in the boxes the name of layer X and the name of layer Y.   *(2 marks)*

    ii The overall density of the Earth is about 5500 kg/m³. The average density of the rocks in the Earth's crust is about 2800 kg/m³. What does this suggest about the material that makes up the lower layers of the Earth?

....

....

....

(2 marks)

  b) In 1915, the scientist Alfred Wegener suggested that Africa and South Africa had once been joined but had since drifted apart. Evidence for his theory came from the animal fossils found in the two continents. The fossils are almost the same, although animals now living in Africa and South America are different. Other scientists did not agree with Wegener and suggested that a land bridge had once joined the two continents.

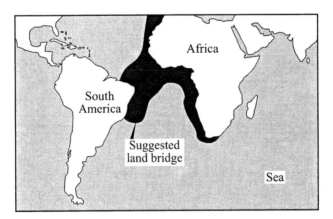

How could scientists use the idea of a land bridge to explain the evidence put forward by Wegener?

....

....

....

(2 marks)

c) Scientists now think that the outer layer of the Earth is cracked into a number of large pieces called tectonic plates. The tectonic plates are moving very slowly. The lines on the map show the boundaries between the major tectonic plates.

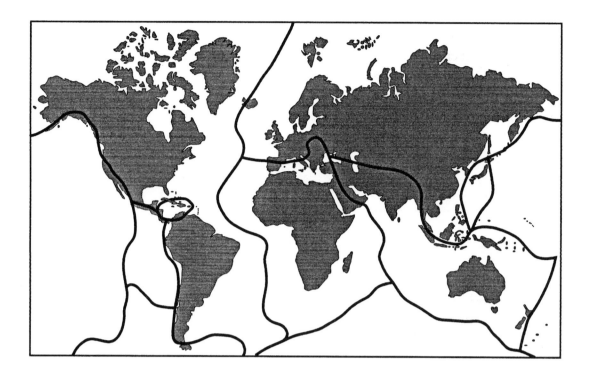

i Explain why there are no major earthquakes in Britain.

....

....

....

(2 marks)

ii What is causing the tectonic plates to move?

....

....

....

(1 mark)

d) i Which parts of the Earth make up its lithosphere?

....

....

(2 marks)

ii Which **two** metals are found at the centre of the Earth?

....

(2 marks)

iii In which state are the metals found at the centre of the Earth.
    Circle the correct answer.

solid   **liquid**   **gas**   *(1 mark)*

9 Chemical calculations

Chemists use a large number (6.02×10^{23}) called the **mole** when 'counting' atoms by weighing them out. They know the relative masses of each element and this is called the relative atomic mass (given the symbol A_r).

D

To work out how many atoms are present in a given mass:

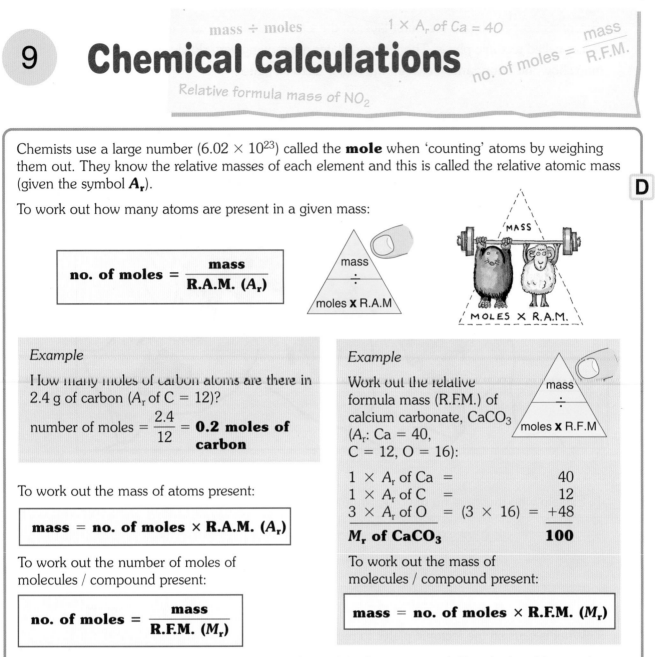

$$\text{no. of moles} = \frac{\text{mass}}{\text{R.A.M. } (A_r)}$$

Example

How many moles of carbon atoms are there in 2.4 g of carbon (A_r of C = 12)?

number of moles $= \dfrac{2.4}{12} =$ **0.2 moles of carbon**

To work out the mass of atoms present:

$$\text{mass} = \text{no. of moles} \times \text{R.A.M. } (A_r)$$

To work out the number of moles of molecules / compound present:

$$\text{no. of moles} = \frac{\text{mass}}{\text{R.F.M. } (M_r)}$$

Example

Work out the relative formula mass (R.F.M.) of calcium carbonate, $CaCO_3$ (A_r: Ca = 40, C = 12, O = 16):

$1 \times A_r$ of Ca =		40
$1 \times A_r$ of C =		12
$3 \times A_r$ of O =	(3×16) =	+48
M_r of $CaCO_3$		100

To work out the mass of molecules / compound present:

$$\text{mass} = \text{no. of moles} \times \text{R.F.M. } (M_r)$$

where M_r **is the relative formula mass (R.F.M.)** of a compound. To calculate M_r, simply ***add up*** all the relative atomic masses of the elements in the compound.

D **H**

▶ **Formulae**

* The simplest ratio of the numbers of moles of each element present in a compound is called its **empirical formula.**
* The actual number of atoms of each element present in a molecule is called its **molecular formula**.
* The **percentage composition** of a compound gives us the proportion of each element present by mass, expressed in percentages (from which we can calculate the empirical formula).

$$\text{percentage of an element in a compound}$$
$$= \frac{\text{mass of that element in 1 mole of the compound}}{\text{relative formula mass of the compound}} \times 100$$

Example

What is the percentage by mass of nitrogen in nitrogen dioxide, NO_2 (A_r of N = 14, O = 16)?

Mass of N in one mole of NO_2 = 14 g

Relative formula mass of NO_2 = $14 + (2 \times 16)$
= 46 g

% of N in NO_2 = $\left(\frac{14}{46}\right) \times 100 = 30.4\%$

▷ Moles of gas

Any gas, at the same temperature and pressure, contains the same number of moles of gas.

- At 20 °C and at a pressure of 1 atmosphere, 1 mole of any gas occupies 24 000 cm^3 (24 dm^3). This information is always given to you in exam questions.

  To work out the number of moles of gas in a given volume:

number of moles of gas

$$= \frac{\text{volume of gas (in cm}^3\text{)}}{24\,000 \text{ cm}^3}$$

or

number of moles of gas

$$= \frac{\text{volume of gas (in dm}^3\text{)}}{24 \text{ dm}^3}$$

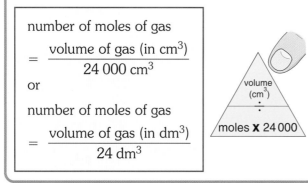

volume (cm^3)

moles **X** 24 000

▷ Calculations involving electrolysis

Given information about one product formed at an electrode during electrolysis, we can predict how much product is formed at the other electrode.

Example

If 4.6 g of sodium (Na) is formed at the cathode in the electrolysis of molten sodium chloride, what volume of chlorine gas is produced at the anode (A_r of Na = 23 and 1 mole of any gas at 20 °C occupies 24 000 cm^3)?

The **half equations** are:

Cathode (−): $Na^+ + e^- \longrightarrow Na$
Anode (+): $2Cl^- - 2e^- \longrightarrow Cl_2$

During the electrolysis the *same number* of electrons must be flowing around the circuit, so we can re-write the half-equation at the cathode as:

$2Na^+ + 2e^- \longrightarrow 2Na$

Therefore if we have 46 g (2 moles) of Na produced, we get 24 000 cm^3 (1 mole) of Cl_2 gas.

So 4.6 g will give **2400 cm^3 of chlorine gas.**

▷ Calculations using balanced equations

Given a balanced equation, we can predict the masses (or volumes of any gases) involved in the chemical reaction.

Example

What volume of oxygen gas (measured at 20 °C) is given off when 8.5 g of sodium nitrate undergoes complete thermal decomposition according to the equation below (A_r of Na = 23, N = 14, O = 16 and 1 mole of any gas at 20 °C occupies 24 000 cm^3)?

$$2NaNO_3(s) \longrightarrow 2NaNO_2(s) + O_2(g)$$

The equation tells us that:

2 moles of $NaNO_3$ will give us 1 mole (24 000 cm^3) of oxygen gas.

The relative formula mass of $NaNO_3 = 23 + 14 + (3 \times 16) = 85$

Therefore 170 g (2 moles) of $NaNO_3$ will give 24 000 cm^3 of oxygen gas.

So 1 g of $NaNO_3$ will give

$$\frac{24\,000}{170} \text{ cm}^3 \text{ of oxygen gas}$$

and 8.5 g of $NaNO_3$ will give

$$\left(\frac{24\,000}{170}\right) \times 8.5 \text{ cm}^3 \text{ of oxygen gas.}$$

This gives: **1200 cm^3 of oxygen gas**

▷ Titrations   Triple Award

We can measure the volume of acid and alkali that neutralise each other using titration and a suitable indicator.

The concentration of a solution is given in **moles per dm^3 (mol dm^{-3})**.

To work out how many moles are in a certain volume of a solution with a known concentration, use this equation:

number of moles in a solution

$$= \text{its concentration} \times \left(\frac{\text{volume of solution in cm}^3}{1000}\right)$$

We can work out the concentration of unknown solutions using the technique of **titration**.

The **balanced equation** tells us the ratio of the numbers of moles of reactants involved in the titration reaction. Then we can use the fact that concentrations are expressed in moles per dm^3 (mol dm^{-3}) to give the answer.

More in *Chemistry for You*, pages 35, 352–75.

Examination Questions – Chemical calculations

1 Aluminium ore contains aluminium oxide.

Marks

   a) Calculate the relative formula mass of aluminium oxide, Al_2O_3.

     (Relative atomic masses: Al = 27, O = 16)

....

....

Answer = ...

(*2 marks*)

   b) Calculate the percentage by mass of aluminium in aluminium oxide.

....

....

Percentage of aluminium = ... %

(*2 marks*)

   c) Calculate the mass of aluminium that could be extracted from 1000 kg of aluminium oxide.

     Use your answer to part b) to help you with this calculation.

....

....

Mass of aluminium = ... kg

(*2 marks*)   6

2 Six thousand five hundred years ago copper ore was smelted to make copper.

   a) Copper pyrites is a type of copper ore.

     Calculate the relative formula mass of copper pyrites, $CuFeS_2$.

     (Relative atomic masses: S = 32, Fe = 56, Cu = 64)

....

....

....

....

(*1 mark*)

   b) Use your answer to part a) to help you calculate the percentage by mass of copper present in copper pyrites, $CuFeS_2$.

....

....

(*2 marks*)   3

3 The trout in a small lake were dying because the water was too acidic.

Limestone, $CaCO_3$, can be used to neutralise the acid.

The equation for the reaction is:

$$CaCO_3 + H_2SO_4 \longrightarrow CaSO_4 + H_2O + CO_2$$

4900 kg of sulphuric acid in the lake needed to be neutralised.

Calculate the mass of limestone, $CaCO_3$, which reacts with this amount of sulphuric acid.

You should show **all** your working.

(Relative atomic masses: H = 1, C = 12, O = 16, S = 32, Ca = 40)

....

....

....

....

....

....

(*3 marks*) 3

4 A nitrogen oxide is produced by microbes in soil.

A sample of this oxide was found to contain 0.56 kg of nitrogen and 0.32 kg of oxygen.

Calculate the empirical formula of this nitrogen oxide.

You must show **all** your working to gain full marks.

(Relative atomic masses: N = 14, O = 16)

....

....

....

....

....

....

(*4 marks*) 4

45

Getting the Grades – Changing materials

Try this question, then compare your answer with the two examples opposite ▶

1 The diagram shows what happens when a sample of limestone (calcium carbonate) is heated then undergoes further reaction. Some of the names are missing.

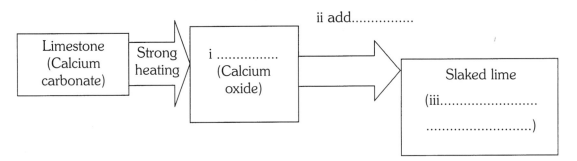

ii add...............

a) Fill in the missing names on the diagram.   (3 marks)

b) Bottles of slaked lime are labelled with the following hazard symbol.

   Why does the slaked lime need to be labelled in this way ?

   ....
   ....
   .... (2 marks)

c) When more water is added to a sample of slaked lime and then filtered, the solution obtained is called limewater. If a student then blows gently through the solution, calcium carbonate is produced and the limewater turns cloudy.

   i What is the name of the gas which reacts to make the limewater cloudy?
   .... (1 mark)

   ii Write a word equation for the reaction which turns the limewater cloudy
   .... (2 marks)

   In certain areas, limestone is crushed to a powder and added to help neutralise soil and the water in lakes which have been affected by acid rain.

d) Why is it preferable to use limestone rather than slaked lime for this process?

   ....
   .... (2 marks)

[Total 10 marks]

GRADE 'A' ANSWER

1 a)   i   Quicklime ✓
         ii   Water ✓
        iii   Calcium hydroxide ✓

   b)   The Hazard sign has a letter 'i' on it to
             indicate an irritant. ✓
             Slaked lime is an alkali and thus will be an
             irritant to the skin ✓

   c)   i   Carbon dioxide ✓
        ii   Calcium hydroxide + carbon dioxide ✓
             ⟶ calcium carbonate ✓ (+ water)

   d)   The calcium carbonate in limestone
             neutralises the acid in the soil or in the
             lakes ✓

The second product, water is not necessary for the second mark

The candidate has not explained why limestone is better than slaked lime. Any excess slaked lime will dissolve to give a harmful alkaline solution. Limestone is not soluble in water

9 marks = Grade A answer

▶ Improve your Grades   A up to A*

Write out and learn the equations for the reactions involved in the following sequence:

Limestone → quicklime → slaked lime → limewater → limestone
$CaCO_3$ → CaO → $Ca(OH)_2(s)$ → $Ca(OH)_2(aq)$ → $CaCO_3$

GRADE 'C' ANSWER

1 a)   i   Quicklime ✓
         ii   Water ✓
        iii   Calcium hydride ✗

   b)   The Hazard sign has a letter 'i' on it to
             indicate that Slaked lime is an
             irritant. ✓ ✗

   c)   i   Carbon dioxide ✓
        ii   Calcium oxide + carbon dioxide ✗
             ⟶ calcium carbonate ✓ (+ water)

   d)   The limestone neutralises the acid
             in the soil or in the lakes ✓

The candidate has (in part iii) missed the fact that oxygen is also present in this compound – thus calcium hydroxide is formed

The candidate has put down the wrong chemical name for slaked lime

The candidate has not mentioned the fact that it is the alkalinity of the slaked lime which makes it an irritant

The candidate has not explained why limestone is better than slaked lime

6 marks = Grade C answer

▶ Improve your Grades   C up to B

Construct a table with three columns and three headings:

Common name	chemical name	chemical formula	comments
Limestone			
Quicklime			
Slaked lime			

Try to complete the table from memory. If you need to, consult your notes or text book.

Examination Questions – The Periodic Table

1   Use the periodic table on the Data Sheet (*see* page 102) to answer these questions.

The table below gives the electronic structures of four elements, **W**, **X**, **Y** and **Z**.

Element	Electronic structure
W	2,5
X	2,7
Y	2,8,8
Z	2,8,8,1

a) Which element **W**, **X**, **Y** or **Z**:

   i   Is a Group 0 gas? ....

   ii Is nitrogen? ....

   iii Is a Group 7 gas? ....

   iv Reacts violently with water? ....   *(2 marks)*

b) Which **two** Groups of the periodic table do **not** contain any metals?

   ....

   (2 marks)   4

2   The picture shows part of a "Chemical Elements" tie, manufactured by "Scienceshirts".

Look at the picture of the tie and then compare it with the Periodic Table on page 102.

a) What do the numbers on the tie represent?

   .... *(1 mark)*

b) In the modern Periodic Table the elements are arranged in Groups.

   Why is this arrangement more useful than the arrangement in Columns on the tie?

   ....

   ....

   ....

   .... *(1 mark)*

c) Choose from **Column F** of the tie the symbol of an element which:

   i   is in Group 2 of the modern Periodic Table; ....

   ii   is a noble gas; ....

   iii is an alkali metal; ....

   iv   has atoms with an electron arrangement, 2,8,5; ....

   v   is not included in the Periodic Table on page 102. ....

   (5 marks)   7

A	B	C	D	E	F	G
B	H (1)	He (2)	Li (3)	Be (4)	B (5)	H (1)
(H)e	C (6)	N (7)	O (8)	F (9)	Ne (10)	C (6)
P	Na (11)	Mg (12)	Al (13)	Si (14)	P (15)	Na (11)
(C)a	S (16)	Cl (17)	Ar (18)	K (19)	Ca (20)	S (16)
(M)n	Sc (21)	Ti (22)	V (23)	Cr (24)	Mn (25)	Sc (21)
Zn	Fe (26)	Co (27)	Ni (28)	Cu (29)	Zn (30)	Fe (26)
Br	Ga (31)	Ge (32)	As (33)	Se (34)	Br (35)	Ga (31)
Zr	Kr (36)	Rb (37)	Sr (38)	Y (39)	Zr (40)	Kr (36)
Rh	Nb (41)	Mo (42)	Tc (43)	Ru (44)	Rh (45)	Nb (41)
Sn	Pd (46)	Ag (47)	Cd (48)	In (49)	Sn (50)	Pd (46)
Cs	Sb (51)	Te (52)	I (53)	Xe (54)	Cs (55)	Sb (51)
Nd	Ba (56)	La (57)	Ce (58)	Pr (59)	Nd (60)	Ba (56)
Tb	Pm (61)	Sm (62)	Eu (63)	Gd (64)	Tb (65)	Pm (61)
Yb	Dy (66)	Ho (67)	Er (68)	Tm (69)	Yb (70)	Dy (66)
Re	Lu (71)	Hf (72)	Ta (73)	W (74)	Re (75)	Lu (71)
Hg	Os (76)	Ir (77)	Pt (78)	Au (79)	Hg (80)	Os (76)
At	Tl (81)	Pb (82)	Bi (83)	Po (84)	At (85)	Tl (81)
Th	Rn (86)	Fr (87)	Ra (88)	Ac (89)	Th (90)	Rn (86)
Am	Pa (91)	U (92)	Np (93)	Pu (94)	Am (95)	Pa (91)
Fm	Cm (96)	Bk (97)	Cf (98)	Es (99)	Fm (100)	Cm (96)
Ha	Md (101)	No (102)	Lr (103)	Rf (104)	Ha (105)	Md (101)
	H (1)	He (2)	Li (3)	Be (4)	B (5)	
	N (7)	O (8)	F (9)			
	Al (13)	(14)				

11 Acids, alkalis and salts

▶ **ThinkAbout:**

1 What is the name of the indicator we use to find the pH of a solution?
2 What is the colour of the indicator in question 1 in:
   a) a strongly acidic solution
   b) a strongly alkaline solution
   c) a neutral solution?

3 What is the pH of a neutral solution?
4 We can extract salt from rock salt. Put the steps below into the correct order:
   A Evaporate off the water.
   B Add water, stir.
   C Crush the rock salt.
   D Filter the mixture.

▶ **Neutralisation**

We can **neutralise** an acid by reacting it with a base. Alkalis are bases that can dissolve in water.
Acids form **hydrogen ions**, $H^+(aq)$, and alkalis form **hydroxide ions**, $OH^-(aq)$.
The general equation for a neutralisation reaction is:

> **acid + a base (or alkali) ⟶ a salt + water**

For example,

hydrochloric acid + sodium hydroxide ⟶ sodium chloride + water
$HCl(aq)$ + $NaOH(aq)$ ⟶ $NaCl(aq)$ + $H_2O(l)$

H

▶ **Ionic equations**

We can summarise what happens when an acid and alkali neutralise each other with an ionic equation:

$$H^+(aq) + OH^-(aq) \longrightarrow H_2O(l)$$

An ionic equation only shows the ions that change in the reaction.

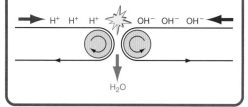

▶ **Preparing salts**

We can make crystals of metal salts from acids.

With an insoluble base, such as a transition metal oxide or hydroxide (e.g. copper oxide), we can filter off the excess base after the acid has been neutralised.

Then we evaporate off some of the water from the salt solution and leave it long enough for the crystals to form.

With an alkali we have to use an indicator to see when the acid has been neutralised.

More in **Chemistry for You,** pages 118–26, 142– 58, 268.

▶ **Salts**

The salt made when we neutralise an acid depends on:
• the acid used, and
• the metal in the base or alkali.

The salt gets the first part of its name from the metal. The last part of its name comes from the acid.

> Hydrochloric acid (HCl) makes salts called **chlorides**.
> Nitric acid (HNO_3) makes salts called **nitrates**.
> Sulphuric acid (H_2SO_4) makes salts called **sulphates**.

E.g.   **zinc nitrate**
     metal   from acid

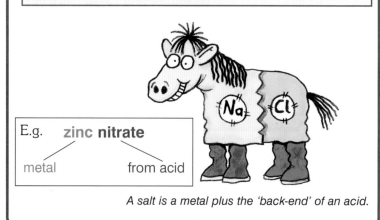

A salt is a metal plus the 'back-end' of an acid.

Answers: **1** universal indicator   **2** a) red   b) purple   c) green   **3** 7   **4** C, B, D, then A

▶ Sodium chloride – common salt

D

We find sodium chloride naturally in the sea and underground as rock salt. It can be pumped up from underground as **brine** (salt solution).

> The brine is electrolysed in industry to form **hydrogen, chlorine** and **sodium hydroxide** solution.

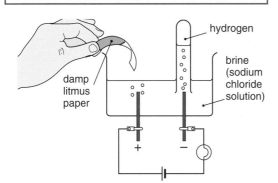

- Hydrogen is given off from the negative electrode.
  (Hydrogen makes a 'pop' – a squeaky explosion – with a lighted splint).

- Chlorine gas is given off from the positive electrode.
  (Chlorine bleaches damp litmus paper).

▶ More salts – silver halides

D

Silver halides are used in photographic film and paper.

They are broken down and reduced to silver by light, X-rays or radioactivity.

e.g.

$$\text{silver bromide} \xrightarrow{\text{light}} \text{silver} + \text{bromine}$$
$$2AgBr \longrightarrow 2Ag + Br_2$$

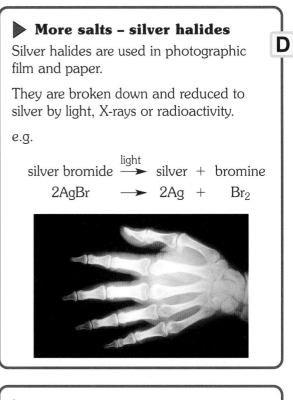

▶ More acids – the hydrogen halides

D

- Hydrogen halides, e.g. HCl, HBr and HI, are gases.
- They dissolve in water to form **acidic solutions**.
- For example, hydrogen chloride gas dissolves in water to form hydrochloric acid.

▶ Useful products from sodium chloride

D

Chlorine
- kills bacteria in swimming pools and in drinking water
- manufacture of hydrochloric acid, disinfectant, bleach and PVC

Hydrogen
- making margarine
- manufacture of ammonia to make fertilisers

Sodium hydroxide
- manufacture of paper and ceramics
- making soap, disinfectants and bleach

▶ Displacement reactions

A more reactive halogen can displace a less reactive halogen from a solution of its halide salt.

E.g.

$$\text{bromine} + \text{sodium iodide} \longrightarrow \text{sodium bromide} + \text{iodine}$$
$$Br_2(aq) + 2\,NaI(aq) \longrightarrow 2\,NaBr(aq) + I_2(aq)$$

Bromine displaces iodide ions from solution. This shows that bromine is more reactive than iodine.

Look at another example:

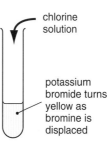

chlorine solution

potassium bromide turns yellow as bromine is displaced

Examination Questions – Acids, alkalis and salts

1 Four solutions, **A, B, C** and **D** are tested with universal indicator.

The table shows the results of these tests.

Solution	pH
A	5–6
B	13–14
C	7
D	1

Marks

a) Which solution is:

i alkaline? ....

ii most strongly acidic? ....

iii weakly acidic? ....

(3 marks)

b) Solution **B** is added to solution **D** until the indicator is green.

i What does this tell you about the mixture of **B** and **D**? Underline the correct answer.

strongly acidic   **weakly acidic**   **neutral**

weakly alkaline   **strongly alkaline**

(1 mark)

ii What do we call the type of reaction between solution **B** and solution **D**?

....

(1 mark)

iii What **two** new substances are produced when solutions **B** and **D** are mixed?

....

and

....

(2 marks)   7

2 Use the Formula of Some Common Ions table on page 101 to help you to answer this question. Acids react with alkalis to form salts and water

Complete the table on page 55 by writing in the name and the formula of the sallt formed in each reaction.

The first one has been done for you.

Acid	Alkali	Salt	Formula of salt
Hydrochloric acid	Sodium hydroxide	Sodium chloride	NaCl
Nitric acid	Sodium hydroxide		
Sulphuric acid	Potassium hydroxide		

(4 marks)   4

3   This question is about the reaction of magnesium metal with acids.

The diagram shows one way of reacting magnesium metal with hydrochloric acid.

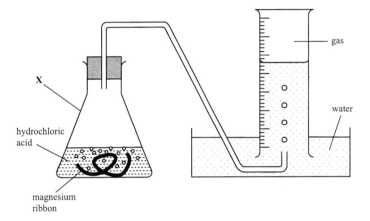

a) Name the piece of apparatus labelled X.

.... *(1 mark)*

b) What is the name of the gas collecting in the measuring cylinder?

.... *(1 mark)*

c) In this reaction a salt is produced. What is the name of the salt?

.... *(1 mark)*

d) Write a word equation for the reaction between magnesium and hydrochloric acid

.... *(1 mark)*

e) In the reaction shown, the bubbles of gas stopped when the measuring cyclinder was half full, and the magnesium ribbon had disappeared. There was still some acid left in X.

i   How could you continue the reaction to ensure that the rest of the acid is used up to produce a neutral solution of the salt?

....

.... *(2 marks)*

ii   How could you obtain a reasonably pure solid sample of the salt produced in this reaction?

....

....

.... *(3 marks)*

f) The salt produced depends upon the acid used. What acid would you use to produce a sample of magnesium nitrate?

.... *(1 mark)*   10

12

Rates of Reaction

▶ ThinkAbout:

1 Which of these factors will increase the rate of a reaction?
   A lowering the temperature
   B increasing the temperature
   C increasing the concentration of solutions
   D decreasing the concentration of solutions.

2 Which gas is given off when limestone reacts with dilute hydrochloric acid?

3 Which gas is given off when magnesium reacts with dilute sulphuric acid?

4 Name a chemical reaction that takes place:
   a) very slowly
   b) very quickly.

▶ Measuring rates of reaction

We can measure rates of reaction by looking at how quickly products are formed.
We can also measure how quickly reactants are used up.

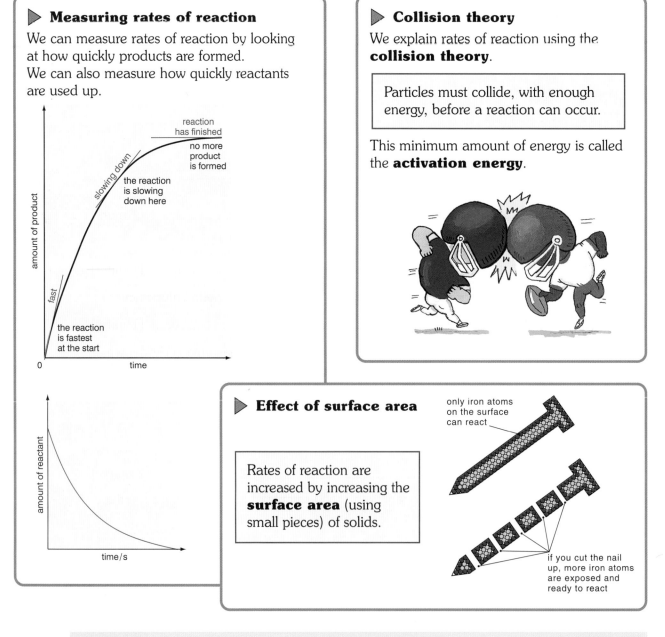

reaction has finished
no more product is formed
the reaction is slowing down here
slowing down
the reaction is fastest at the start
fast
amount of product
0   time

amount of reactant
time/s

▶ Collision theory

We explain rates of reaction using the **collision theory**.

Particles must collide, with enough energy, before a reaction can occur.

This minimum amount of energy is called the **activation energy**.

▶ Effect of surface area

Rates of reaction are increased by increasing the **surface area** (using small pieces) of solids.

only iron atoms on the surface can react

if you cut the nail up, more iron atoms are exposed and ready to react

Answers:
1 B and C   2 carbon dioxide   3 hydrogen   4 a) e.g. iron rusting/concrete setting
b) e.g. dynamite exploding / acid neutralising an alkali

56

▶ Effect of concentration

> Rates of reaction are increased by increasing the **concentration** of solutions.

acid particles

marble chip

If this is a 1M solution of acid . . . . . . .this is a 2M solution. There are twice as many acid particles **in the same volume of solution**

When we increase the concentration (or pressure in gas reactions), there are more particles in the same space so particles collide more often.

> **Take care:**
> When explaining the effect of concentration, don't just say that there are more particles – explain that there are more particles *in a given volume* and therefore more collisions *in a given time*.

> Rates of reaction are increased by increasing the **pressure** of gases.

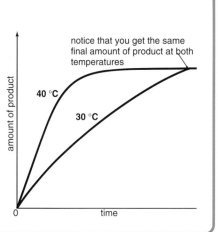

increase pressure

sealed syringe

▶ Effect of temperature

> Rates of reaction are increased by increasing the **temperature**.

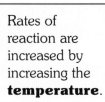 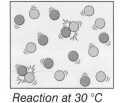 

Reaction at 30 °C   *Reaction at 40 °C*

When we increase the temperature, the reacting particles gain more energy:
- They move around faster, so collisions are **more frequent**.
- The collisions are also **more energetic,** so are more likely to produce a reaction (more reacting particles will have energy that exceeds the **activation energy** for the reaction).

notice that you get the same final amount of product at both temperatures

amount of product

40 °C

30 °C

time

▶ Catalysts

> Rates of reaction are increased by using a **catalyst.** (That is, if you can find one for a particular reaction, as different reactions need different catalysts.)

over we go!

NO CATALYST

WITH CATALYST

A catalyst can be used over and over again as it is not chemically changed itself at the end of the reaction.

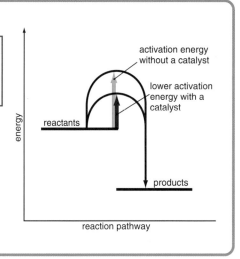

activation energy without a catalyst

lower activation energy with a catalyst

energy

reactants

products

reaction pathway

More in *Chemistry for You*, pages 199–211.

Examination Questions – Rates of reaction

1 Some students investigate the rate of the reaction between magnesium and dilute hydrochloric acid.

They use 0.1 g of magnesium **ribbon** and measure the volume of hydrogen produced at 30 second intervals.

The reaction ends when all the magnesium is used up.

The results are shown on the graph.

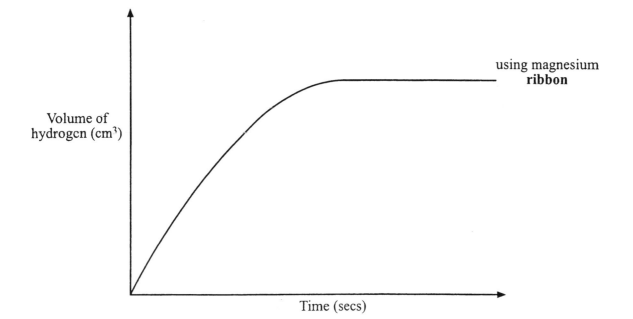

The students do the experiment again. This time they use the same volume of the same acid but with 0.1 g of magnesium **powder**.

Marks

a) On the graph above, sketch the curve you would expect the students to obtain.

(2 marks)

b) The rate of reaction between magnesium and hydrochloric acid is greater if the concentration of the acid is increased.

Explain why, in terms of particles.

....

....

....

(2 marks)

c) When the reaction is finished, a solution of magnesium chloride is left behind.
Write a word equation for the reaction between magnesium and hydrochloric acid.

.... + ... ⟶ .... + ...

(2 marks)

6

2 Calcium carbonate reacts with dilute nitric acid to produce carbon dioxide.

$$CaCO_3 + 2HNO_3 \longrightarrow Ca(NO_3)_2 + H_2O + CO_2$$

A 10 g lump of calcium carbonate was reacted with 20 cm³ of dilute nitric acid. When the reaction was finished, some of the calcium carbonate was left unreacted. The graph shows the volume of carbon dioxide made in each minute for sixteen minutes.

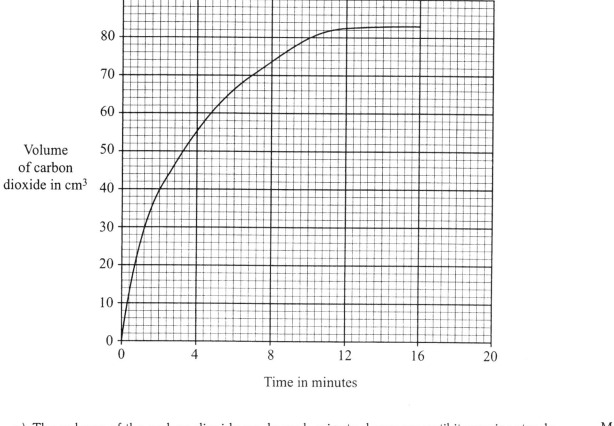

a) The volume of the carbon dioxide made each minute decreases until it remains steady at 83 cm³

   Explain why.

   ....

   ....

   ....

   ....

   (2 marks)

b) Draw a line, on the axes above, for an experiment where 20 cm³ of the same dilute nitric acid was reacted with 10 g of powdered calcium carbonate.

   (2 marks)

c) Give **one** way of changing the rate of this reaction (other than using powdered calcium carbonate).

   ....

   ....

   ....

   (1 mark)

Marks

5

59

Enzymes

13

D

▷ **ThinkAbout:**

1 How are enzymes used in your digestive system?

2 Are the conditions in your stomach acidic, alkaline or neutral?

3 At which temperature are the enzymes in your body likely to work best?
A 0 °C   B 20 °C   C 40 °C   D 60 °C

4 How could you test that the gas given off during fermentation is carbon dioxide?

▷ **How enzymes work**

The chemical reactions in living cells are catalysed by **enzymes**.

> Enzymes are called **biological catalysts**.
> They are large **protein** molecules.

Their special complex shapes match the molecules they help to react.

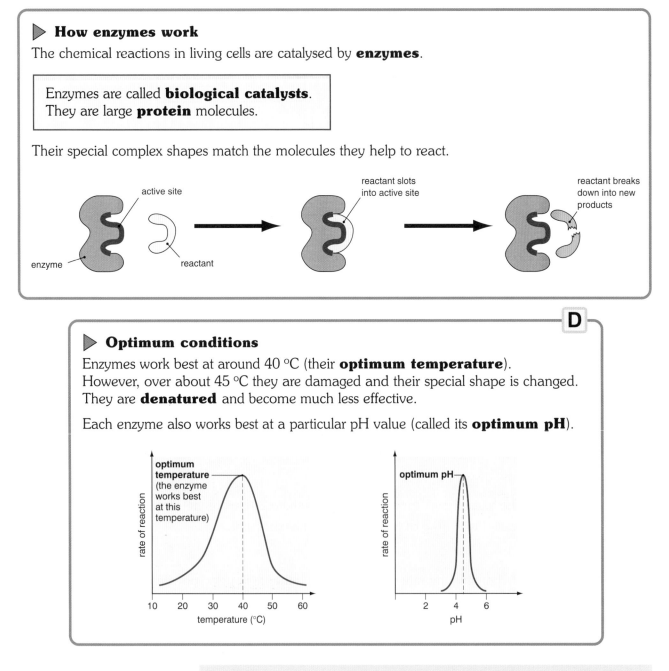

▷ **Optimum conditions**

Enzymes work best at around 40 °C (their **optimum temperature**).
However, over about 45 °C they are damaged and their special shape is changed.
They are **denatured** and become much less effective.

Each enzyme also works best at a particular pH value (called its **optimum pH**).

Answers:

1 to break down large food molecules   **2** acidic   **3** C, 40 °C
4 bubble the gas into limewater which will turn milky

▷ Fermentation

Fermentation is the reaction in which yeast cells convert sugar (glucose) into alcohol (ethanol) and carbon dioxide gas:

$$\text{sugar} \xrightarrow{\text{enzymes in yeast}} \text{alcohol} + \text{carbon dioxide}$$
$$\text{(glucose)} \qquad\qquad \text{(ethanol)}$$

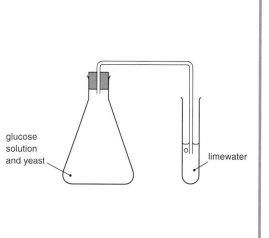

glucose solution and yeast

limewater

The reaction is catalysed by enzymes in the yeast cells, in the absence of oxygen.

We use fermentation to make:
- the alcohol in wine and beer
- the bubbles (of carbon dioxide) that make bread dough rise.

▷ Other uses of enzymes

Enzymes can save energy costs in industry because reactions can take place at relatively low temperatures. Researchers are finding more and more uses.

For example, enzymes are used:
- in biological washing powders and liquids to break down stains
- in some baby foods to 'pre-digest' proteins
- to change starch syrup into sugar syrup
- to convert glucose into the less fattening sugar called fructose
- to make yoghurt (changing lactose, a sugar, in milk into lactic acid).

▷ Techniques in biotechnology

Scientists have had to find ways to use enzymes to greatest effect and have found how to:
- keep enzymes active for longer periods
- immobilise the enzymes by trapping them in an inert support or on carrier beads (of calcium alginate).

These techniques make the process of making the new substance **continuous**, rather than the **batch process** used in traditional enzyme reactions, such as brewing.

Help!

Let us out!

H

Take care:
- Enzymes are molecules found *in* living things.
- They are not living things themselves, so they *cannot* be killed!

More in **Chemistry for You**, pages 212–19.

Examination Questions – Enzymes

1 Living cells are used to make beer and yoghurt.

   a) Complete each sentence by using the correct words from the box.

alcohol	fructose	lactic acid	milk sugar
oxygen	protein	starch	sugar

   In beer-making, yeast converts .... into carbon dioxide and ....

   In yoghurt-making, bacteria convert .... into ....

   (4 marks)

   b) Describe the test for carbon dioxide.

   ....

   ....

   ....

   (2 marks)   6

2 We can use yeast to change sugar into alcohol and carbon dioxide. This process is called fermentation.

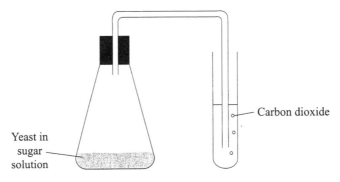

Yeast in sugar solution

Carbon dioxide

   a) Complete the sentences by choosing the correct words from the box.

bread	cheese	wine	yoghurt

   Alcohol produced in this way is used in making ....

   Carbon dioxide produced by fermentation can be used to make .... rise.

   (2 marks)

   b) Three test tubes were set up, as shown below. The temperature was kept at 15 °C.

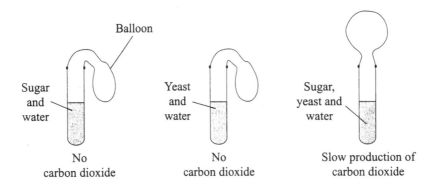

Balloon

| Sugar and water | Yeast and water | Sugar, yeast and water |
| No carbon dioxide | No carbon dioxide | Slow production of carbon dioxide |

i Give **one** advantage of using enzymes in chemical reactions.

....

.... *(1 mark)*

ii Give **one** disadvantage of using enzymes in chemical reactions.

....

.... *(1 mark)*   4

3 The diagram shows how a beer called Newcastle Brown Ale is made.

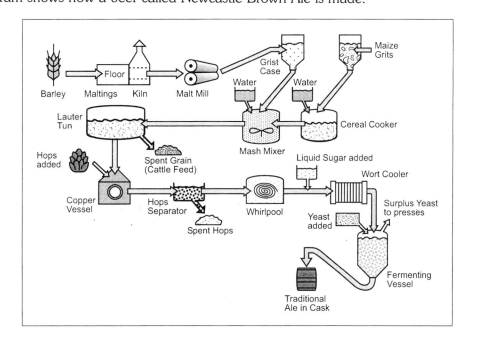

a) Use the diagram to help you to name four of the raw materials used to make this beer.

1. ....   2. ....

3. ....   4. ....

(2 marks)

b) In the Mash Mixer sugars are formed. The reaction is helped by an enzyme.
How does the enzyme help the reaction?

....

.... *(1 mark)*

c) In the fermenting vessel sugars are changed into two products.
One of these is alcohol (ethanol). Name the other product.

.... *(1 mark)*

d) The fermenting vessel is cooled using cold water because the fermentation reaction gives out heat.

i What name is given to reactions that give out heat?

.... *(1 mark)*

ii A solution of sugar containing enzymes must not be allowed to become too hot.
Explain why.

....

.... *(1 mark)*   6

ThinkAbout:

1 What is the main difference between a physical change and a reversible chemical change?

2 What do you see if you add too much acid to an alkaline solution containing universal indicator, and then add too much alkali?

3 a) How can you test for the presence of water using anhydrous copper sulphate?

b) Give another chemical test for the presence of water.

c) How could you show that the liquid was pure water?

D

▷ Examples of reversible reactions

Some reactions are **reversible**.

The reactants form the products, but the products can also react together to re-form the reactants:

reactants $\rightleftharpoons$ products

- The test for water (white anhydrous copper sulphate turns blue) is a reversible reaction.
- The breakdown and formation of ammonium chloride is reversible:

ammonium chloride $\rightleftharpoons$ ammonia + hydrogen chloride

$NH_4Cl(s)$ $\rightleftharpoons$ $NH_3(g)$ + $HCl(g)$

a white solid   *colourless gases*

When the white ammonium chloride powder is heated it decomposes. It gives off ammonia and hydrogen chloride gases. On the cool part of the test tube, the gases re-combine to form the white solid again.

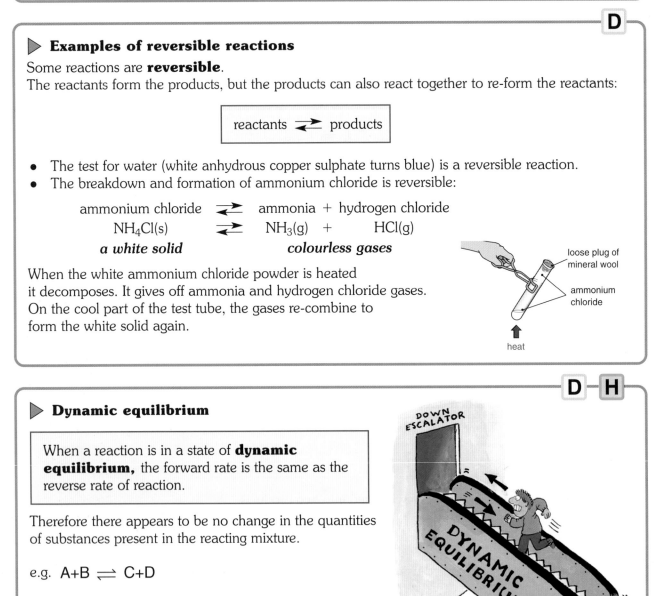

loose plug of mineral wool

ammonium chloride

heat

D **H**

▷ Dynamic equilibrium

When a reaction is in a state of **dynamic equilibrium,** the forward rate is the same as the reverse rate of reaction.

Therefore there appears to be no change in the quantities of substances present in the reacting mixture.

e.g. $A+B \rightleftharpoons C+D$

All four substances (A, B, C and D) will be present in fixed proportions once equilibrium has been reached.

DOWN ESCALATOR

DYNAMIC EQUILIBRIUM

Answers:

1 New substances are formed in reversible chemical changes but not in physical changes.

2 purple → red → purple again **3** a) It turns blue if water is present.

b) Blue cobalt chloride turns pink. c) It would boil at 100 °C.

> The position of equilibrium shifts to *oppose* whatever change we introduce to the system.

The various factors are shown below:

Changing concentration

* *Increasing* the concentration of one of the substances in the equilibrium mixture moves the position of equilibrium to favour the *opposite side*. D H

more A

increasing
concentration of A

A+B ⇌ C+D

equilibrium moves to right to
reduce the concentration of A

Effect of temperature

* *Increasing* the temperature shifts the position of equilibrium to favour the *endothermic reaction*. D H
* *Decreasing* the temperature shifts the position of equilibrium to favour the *exothermic reaction*.

increasing
temperature

A+B ⇌ C+D+ heat

(forward reaction
is exothermic)

equilibrium moves to left to
get rid of the extra heat

Effect of pressure

In reactions involving different numbers of gas molecules on either side of the equation: D H

* *Increasing* the pressure shifts the position of equilibrium to favour the side with the *least number* of gas molecules.
* *Decreasing* the pressure shifts the position of equilibrium to favour the side with the *greater number* of gas molecules.

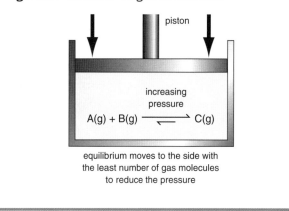

piston

increasing
pressure

A(g) + B(g) ⇌ C(g)

equilibrium moves to the side with
the least number of gas molecules
to reduce the pressure

Take care:

* Reversible reactions in industry are not always carried out at the highest possible temperature.

* If a high temperature favours the reactants, a temperature is chosen that is a compromise between a lower yield and a faster rate of reaction.

▷ **Reversible reactions in industry**

In industrial processes that involve reversible reactions, chemists have to balance the need for a reasonable yield with the need for a fast rate of reaction. For example, in the **Haber process**:

$$N_2(g) + 3H_2(g) \rightleftharpoons 2NH_3(g) \quad \Delta H = -92 \text{ kJ mol}^{-1} \text{ (exothermic in forward direction)}$$ D H

* A low temperature favours a high yield of ammonia, but at a slow rate. So a temperature of 450 °C is chosen as a compromise between yield and rate.
* Iron is used as a catalyst to speed up the rate of reaction. But because it speeds up both the forward and reverse reaction, it doesn't affect the yield of ammonia.

> A **catalyst** speeds up the *rate* at which we reach equilibrium, but does not affect the position of equilibrium.

More in *Chemistry for You*, pages 232–41.

Examination Questions – Reversible reactions

1 A student heated some blue copper sulphate crystals. The crystals turned into white anhydrous copper sulphate.

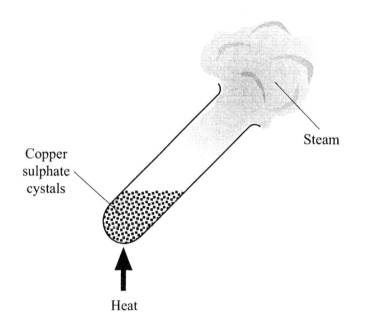

Copper sulphate cystals

Steam

Heat

a) The blue copper sulphate had to be heated to change it into white copper sulphate.

State whether the reaction was exothermic or endothermic.

....

Explain your answer.

....

....

(1 mark)

Marks

b) The word equation for this reaction is shown below.

    hydrated   [+ heat energy] ⇌   anhydrous   + water
  copper sulphate   copper sulphate
     (blue)   (white)

  i What does the symbol ⇌ tell you about this reaction?

....

(1 mark)

  ii How could the student turn the white powder back to blue?

....

(1 mark)

3

2 This question is about the reaction between nitrogen and hydrogen to make the gas ammonia.
   Look carefully at the equation below

Iron catalyst

$N_2(g) + 3H_2(g) \rightleftharpoons 2NH_3(g) \quad \Delta H = -92 \text{ kJmol}^{-1}$

The reaction is a dynamic equilibrium.

a) What symbol shown above is used to represent a dynamic equilibrium?   Marks

....

(1 mark)

The forward reaction in this equilibrium is exothermic.

b) How can you tell that the reaction above is exothermic?

....

(1 mark)

c) Changing conditions such as temperature and pressure can have an effect on the
   position of the equilibrium and therefore the yield of ammonia.

   i What effect will an increase in pressure have upon the position of the equilibrium?

   ....

   ....

(1 mark)

   ii How will an increase in pressure affect the yield of ammonia?

   ....

(1 mark)

   iii How will an increase in temperature affect the yield of ammonia?

   ....

   ....

(2 marks)

In the industrial process the reaction is performed at a temperature between 400 °C and
450 °C.

d) Explain why this temperature is a compromise?

....

....

(2 marks)

e) Particles of finely divided iron are used as a catalyst for this process. Why does the
   catalyst help?

....

....

(2 marks)   10

15

Energy Transfer

▶ ThinkAbout:

1 You are holding the bottom of a beaker containing two solutions that react together in an exothermic reaction. What do you feel?

2 In a reversible reaction, the forward reaction gives out 150 kJ mol⁻¹ of energy. What energy do you think the reverse reaction will take in?

3 Where do we get the energy our bodies need to survive?

4 Do you think we need to put energy into a compound to break its bonds, or do you think energy will be given out in this process?

▶ Exothermic and endothermic reactions

Reactions that give out energy, often as heat, are called **exothermic**.
The temperature of the surroundings rises.

Reactions that take in energy are called **endothermic**. The temperature of the surroundings falls.

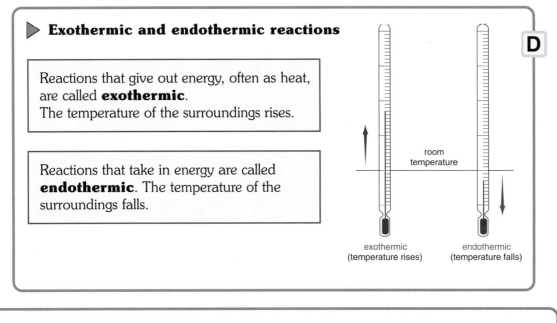

D

room temperature

exothermic
(temperature rises)

endothermic
(temperature falls)

▶ Energy transfer in reversible reactions

In a reversible reaction:
● If the forward reaction is exothermic, the reverse reaction is endothermic.
● If the forward reaction is endothermic, the reverse reaction is exothermic.

In a reversible reaction, the amount of energy given out or taken in will be equal for the forward and reverse reactions.

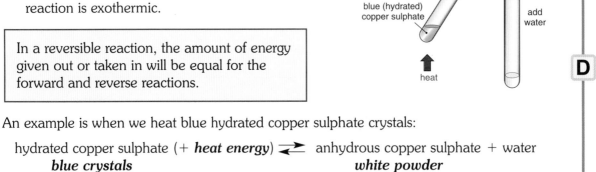

steam

drops of water

blue (hydrated) copper sulphate

add water

heat

D

An example is when we heat blue hydrated copper sulphate crystals:

hydrated copper sulphate (+ **heat energy**) ⇌ anhydrous copper sulphate + water
blue crystals   *white powder*

Answers: **1** It will feel warm/hot.   **2** 150 kJ mol⁻¹   **3** food   **4** put energy in

▷ Energy level diagrams

We can show energy changes in chemical reactions on an energy level diagram.

ΔH is the symbol for the energy change in a reaction.

> **ΔH is negative** for an **exothermic** reaction.

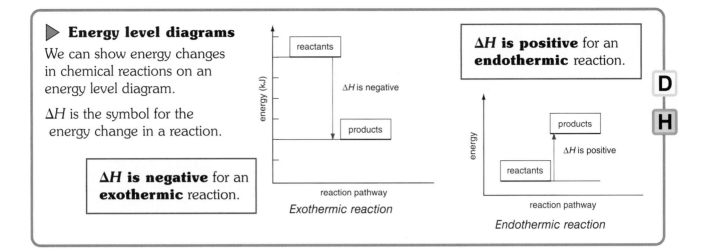

Exothermic reaction

> **ΔH is positive** for an **endothermic** reaction.

Endothermic reaction

D

H

▷ Bond energies

> **Breaking bonds** requires energy. It is an **endothermic** process.

> **Making new bonds** gives out energy. It is an **exothermic** process.

- Bond energies are a measure of the *strength* of a bond.
- We can use bond energies to work out an approximate value of **ΔH** for a reaction.
- If the energy given out when new bonds form is *greater than* the energy needed to break the existing bonds, then the reaction is exothermic.
- If the energy given out when new bonds form is *less than* the energy needed to break the existing bonds, then the reaction is endothermic.

Example

Calculate the approximate energy change accompanying the reaction between hydrogen and chlorine to make hydrogen chloride:

$$H_2 + Cl_2 \longrightarrow 2HCl$$

(Bond energy values are: H—H = 436 kJ mol^{-1}, Cl—Cl = 242 kJ mol^{-1}, H—Cl = 431 kJ mol^{-1})

Bonds broken:

$$+[1 \times (H—H)] + [1 \times (Cl—Cl)]$$
$$= +(436 + 242)$$
$$= +678 \text{ kJ mol}^{-1}$$

Bonds made:

$$-(2 \times H—Cl)$$
$$= -(2 \times 431)$$
$$= -862 \text{ kJ mol}^{-1}$$

Adding these two up to get the overall energy change we get:

$$(+678) + (-862)$$
$$= \mathbf{-184 \text{ kJ mol}^{-1}}$$

D

H

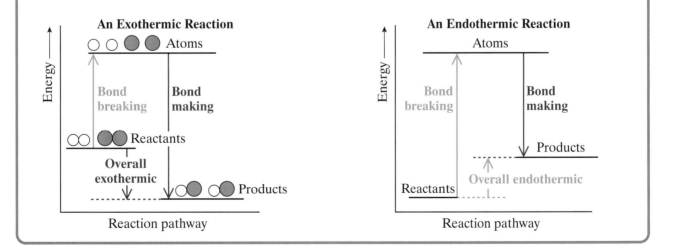

More in *Chemistry for You*, pages 190–97.

Examination Questions – Energy transfer

1 This question is about the reaction between magnesium and hydrochloric acid.

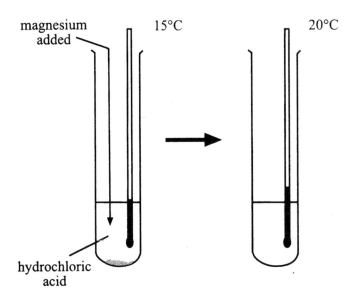

Choose words from the list to complete the sentence below.

endothermic   exothermic   oxidation

obtained from   released as light to   released as heat to

The reaction between magnesium and hydrochloric acid is an ....

reaction because energy is .... the surroundings.

(2 marks)   2

2 Hydrogen will combine with chlorine to produce hydrogen chloride.

The reaction can be represented by this equation.

$$H_2 \quad + \quad Cl_2 \quad \longrightarrow \quad 2HCl$$

$$H-H \quad + \quad Cl-Cl \quad \longrightarrow \quad 2H-Cl$$

a) Show, by calculation, that this reaction is exothermic.
   (All your working should be shown).

Bond	Energy needed to break bonds or released when bonds are formed (kJ per formula mass)
H—H	436
Cl—Cl	240
H—Cl	431

....

....

....

....

....

(3 marks)

b) At room temperature a piece of magnesium ribbon does not burn in chlorine. However, if we light the magnesium ribbon first, then place it in chlorine, it burns with a powerful, white flame.

This exothermic reaction can be represented by a word equation.

$$\text{magnesium } + \text{ chlorine } \longrightarrow \text{ magnesium chloride}$$

Sketch an energy level diagram for the reaction and show on the diagram, the nett energy released.

Energy

Time (secs)

(3 marks)

c) What do we call a reaction that takes in energy from its surroundings?

....

(1 mark)

d) Look at the reaction below (the letters are not chemical symbols):

$$\text{X } + \text{ Y } \longrightarrow \text{ Z}$$

This reaction gives out 125 kJ mol^{-1}

What will be the energy change when Z decomposes to form X and Y?
Will this energy be given out or taken in?

....

(2 marks)   9

Getting the Grades – Patterns of behaviour

Try this question, then compare your answer with the two examples opposite ▶

1 This questions is about some of the important features of the periodic table.

a) Name the blocks which have been labelled :

   i A..

   ii B...

   iii C..

   iv D.. (4 marks)

b) The elements in block A all react in a similar way when added to water.

   i What are the similarities?

   ....

   .... (2 marks)

   ii Give one difference on descending the group.

   ....

   (1 mark)

c) Describe and explain the trend in reactivity of the elements on descending block C.

   i Description of trend.

   ....

   ii Explanation of trend.

   ....

   ....

   .... (4 marks)

d) What is unusual about the chemical properties of the elements in the block labelled D? Explain why they behave in this way.

   ....

   ....

   .... (2 marks)

   [Total 13 marks]

The candidate has not given details of the products, namely hydrogen gas and an alkaline solution

1 a) i Group 1, The Alkali metals ✓
     ii The transition metals ✓
    iii Group 7, the halogens ✓
     iv Group O, the noble gases ✓
  b) i They all dissolve ✓
     ii Their reactivity increases ✓
  c) i The reactivity of the elements decreases
          on descending the group. ✓
     ii The elements react by gaining electrons. ✓
          On descending the group the number of
          electron shells increases. ✓
  d)   These elements will not react readily. ✓
          This is because their atoms have a
          complete outermost shell of electrons ✓

The candidate has not connected the two facts given above – ie The increase in number of shells reduces the attractive effect of the nucleus, thus reducing the reactivity.

11 marks = Grade A answer

▶ Improve your Grades   A up to A*

Part c) of this question is aimed at Grade A candidates. It is important here to explain the effect on reactivity of the increasing number of electron shells in the atom. This same effect underpins all the trends observed on descending groups in the periodic table. On moving across a period the increasing number of protons in the nucleus increase the tendency of the atoms to attract electrons. Thus the trend across a period is from metals to non metals. Bear these two ideas in mind as you look at your annotated copy of the periodic table so you not only remember the trend but also understand the changes in atomic structure which cause them.

The candidate has not given details of the products, namely hydrogen gas and an alkaline solution

1 a) i Group 1, The Alkali metals ✓
     ii The transition metals ✓
    iii Group 7, the halogens ✓
     iv Group O, the noble gases ✓
  b) i They all dissolve ✓
     ii Their reactivity decreases ✗

  c) i The reactivity of the elements decreases
          on descending the group. ✓
     ii The elements react less vigorously
          going down the group. ✗
  d)   These elements do not react ✓

The candidate has the trend the wrong way round

The candidate has not tried to explain the trend – it has just been restated in different words

7 marks = Grade C answer

▶ Improve your Grades   C up to B

The periodic table makes sense of a vast number of chemical reactions and behaviours. In trying to make sense of chemistry it is really helpful to have as many copies of the periodic table as possible. Use arrows and labels to plot all the trends you can on the table.
Pin these up somewhere conspicuous so that the directions of the trends become second nature to you.

16 ORGANIC CHEMISTRY

> ▶ **ThinkAbout:**

1 How many covalent bonds can a carbon atom form?

2 How many covalent bonds can a hydrogen atom form?

3 Which type of reaction do we use to make alcoholic drinks?

4 What do we call the very large molecules made up from thousands of monomers?

> ▶ **Organic molecules**

Organic compounds are based on carbon atoms (although they do not include oxides of carbon, carbonates or hydrogencarbonates). When we burn fossil fuels or wood in a good supply of air, this carbon is oxidised to carbon dioxide and any hydrogen gets oxidised to water. This is called a **combustion** reaction. When complete combustion takes place we get:

methane + oxygen → carbon dioxide + water

If we only have a limited supply of air, we get incomplete combustion, and poisonous **carbon monoxide gas (CO)** is formed. This gas bonds to the **haemoglobin** in the blood and it can no longer carry oxygen around the body, leading to unconsciousness, then death.

We also get tiny solid particles of black carbon formed during incomplete combustion of fossil fuels and other organic compounds.

> ▶ **Isomers** **H**

> **Isomers** are substances with the same chemical formula but *different* arrangements of atoms within their molecules.

Look at the isomers of C_4H_{10} below:

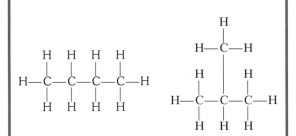

Isomers with branching from their carbon chain have lower boiling points than their straight chain isomer. The more branching, the lower the boiling point (as branched chains cannot pack together as well as straight chains).

> ▶ **Groups of organic compounds**

Groups or families of organic compounds that have the same general formula and undergo similar reactions are called **homologous series**. For example, **H**

- The **alkanes** have the general formula C_nH_{2n+2}.
- The **alkenes** (that contain one double bond) are C_nH_{2n}.

All the alkenes undergo **addition reactions** (in which the double bond breaks and new single bonds form). For example:

$$C_2H_4 + H_2 \xrightarrow{\text{nickel catalyst}} C_2H_6$$

This reaction is used to harden unsaturated oils in the manufacture of margarine.

> ▶ **Alcohols** **H**

The homologous series of **alcohols** all contain the **—OH** grouping. This makes them more reactive than corresponding alkanes. The alcohols also have higher boiling points.

Ethanol (C_2H_5OH) is a member of the alcohol family. It is used in alcoholic drinks, as a fuel and as a solvent.

We can make ethanol by two methods:

Fermenting glucose with yeast

The enzymes in yeast, in the absence of oxygen, break down the glucose:

glucose → ethanol + carbon dioxide

The carbon dioxide gas is allowed to escape, but no air is let in (otherwise the ethanol gets oxidised and tastes sour).

Hydrating ethene with steam 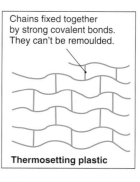 H

This is done under pressure in the presence of a phosphoric(V) acid catalyst:

ethene + steam → ethanol

- The ethanol produced by this second method can be run as a **continuous process** (as opposed to the batch process used in fermentation vats).
- However, the ethanol cannot be used in drinks.
- Also the process does use up a valuable resource in that crude oil is the raw material for ethene (whereas sugar is extracted from plants).

More in **Chemistry for You**, pages 178–85.

▶ General reactions of alcohols H

With sodium metal

alcohol + sodium → sodium salt of the alcohol + hydrogen

Combustion

alcohol + oxygen → carbon dioxide + water

Oxidation

alcohol → carboxylic acid

Esterification

$$\text{alcohol + carboxylic acid} \underset{}{\overset{\text{conc. sulphuric acid}}{\rightleftharpoons}} \text{ester + water}$$

Esters are used in perfumes and in food flavourings.

▶ More about polymers H

There are two types of plastic:

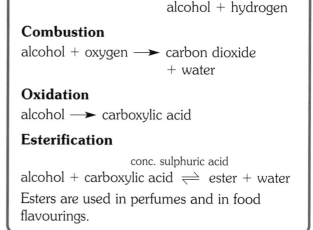

Relatively weak forces between the separate polymer chains. They soften on heating (remouldable).

Thermosoftening plastic

Chains fixed together by strong covalent bonds. They can't be remoulded.

Thermosetting plastic

Burning plastics will reduce the volume of waste in landfill sites.

However, many plastics produce pollution if burned in a limited supply of air. Compounds containing chlorine form acidic hydrogen chloride gas, and those containing nitrogen give off toxic hydrogen cyanide gas.

Carboxylic acids

These are weak acids, found in citrus fruits and soft drinks (as citric acid) and in vinegar (as ethanoic acid). Aspirin is also a carboxylic acid (used to relieve pain and reduce the risk of heart attacks).

Here are the first three members of the homologous series:

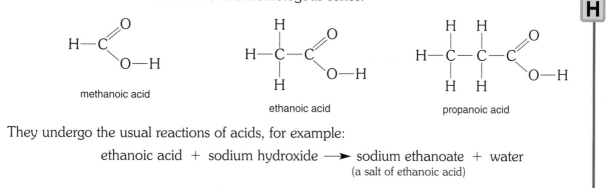

methanoic acid

ethanoic acid

propanoic acid

They undergo the usual reactions of acids, for example:

ethanoic acid + sodium hydroxide → sodium ethanoate + water
(a salt of ethanoic acid)

ethanoic acid + sodium carbonate → sodium ethanoate + water + carbon dioxide

Examination Questions – Organic chemistry

1 Alcohols

This question is about the formation and reactions of an alcohol called ethanol. Ethanol has the formula C_2H_5OH.

Marks

a) Ethanol can be formed by the fermenting of glucose by yeast. The process produces a gas which will turn limewater cloudy.

   i What is the gas produced as a result of the fermentation of glucose?

....

(1 mark)

   ii Write a word equation to represent the fermentation process.

yeast

.... $\longrightarrow$ .... + ...

(1 mark)

b) Ethanol can also be made by reacting ethene gas $C_2H_4(g)$ with steam in the presence of a catalyst of phosphoric(V) acid.

Write a symbol equation for this reaction.

(catalyst of phosphoric acid)

.... + ... $\longrightarrow$ ....

(2 marks)

c) What is the advantage of producing ethanol

   i from ethene?

....

   ii by the fermentation of sugar?

....

(2 marks)

d) The ethanol produced by either method can be used in a variety of ways. Excluding alcoholic drinks, give two uses for ethanol.

....

....

(2 marks)   8

2 Isomers

This question is about isomers.

a) The two molecules drawn on the next page are isomers of the alkane, butane.

   i Which of these two isomers will have the higher boiling point?

....

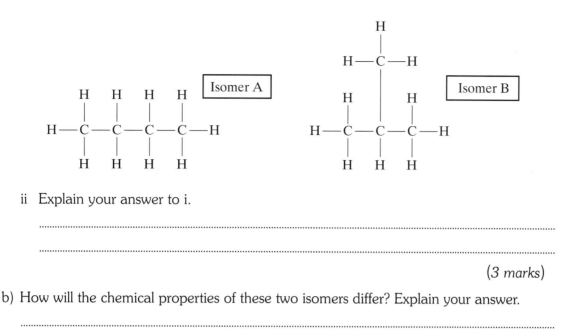

ii Explain your answer to i.

....

....

(3 marks)

b) How will the chemical properties of these two isomers differ? Explain your answer.

....

.... *(2 marks)*   5

3 Carboxylic acids

This question is about carboxylic acids are formed when an alcohol is oxidised.

a) Complete the table below to give the name and formula of each carboxylic acid formed when ethanol and propan-1-ol are oxidised.

Alcohol	Formula	Name of carboxylic acid	Formula of carboxylic acid formed
Methanol	CH_3OH	Methanoic acid	HCOOH
Ethanol	C_2H_5OH		
Propan-1–ol	C_3H_7OH		

(4 marks)

b) How will these acids react with:

i magnesium ribbon? ....

....

ii sodium carbonate solution? ....

.... *(2 marks)*

c) These acids will all react with alcohols in the presence of an acid catalyst to make sweet smelling compounds?

i What is the name for this class of sweet smelling compounds?

....

ii Write a word equation to show the general reaction by which these compounds are made.

.... + ... $\longrightarrow$ .... + ...

(2 marks)

d) What can these compounds be used for?

....

(2 marks)   10

17 Industrial processes

ThinkAbout:

1 What is the chemical symbol of:
  a) aluminium   b) magnesium
  c) iron   d) titanium?

2 What is the chemical formula of:
  a) sulphur dioxide b) sulphur trioxide
  c) sulphuric acid   d) vanadium(V) oxide?

Manufacture of sulphuric acid

Sulphuric acid (H_2SO_4) is manufactured in the **Contact process.**

- First of all, sulphur is burned in air to give sulphur dioxide gas (SO_2).
- Then sulphur dioxide is mixed with more air to yield sulphur trioxide in a reversible reaction.
- A compromise temperature of 450 °C is chosen and the gases are passed through layers of vanadium(V) oxide catalyst (V_2O_5).
- Finally, sulphur trioxide is added to concentrated sulphuric acid making fuming sulphuric acid, which is called **oleum**. Water is carefully added to the oleum to make 98% sulphuric acid.

In effect the reaction is:

$$SO_3(g) + H_2O(l) \longrightarrow H_2SO_4(l)$$

However, if this reaction were to be carried out as shown in the equation, a mist of sulphuric acid forms that is difficult to condense and would pollute the atmosphere.

Some uses of sulphuric acid

Sulphuric acid is used to make **fertilisers** and **detergents**. It is the acid found inside **car batteries**.

Sulphuric acid is also a **dehydrating agent**. This means that it can remove H_2O from molecules in a chemical reaction with some compounds, for example:

sugar $\longrightarrow$ carbon + water

hydrated copper $\rightarrow$ anhydrous copper + water
sulphate   sulphate
(blue crystals)   *(white powder)*

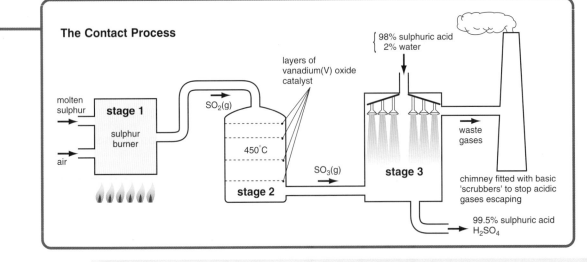

The Contact Process

► Anodising aluminium

Aluminium is quite a reactive metal, yet it resists corrosion. The thin oxide layer that coats aluminium protects it from attack by air and water.

We can improve aluminium's resistance to corrosion even further by making the oxide layer thicker. In industry this is done by **anodising** the aluminium.
- The first step is to remove the existing layer of aluminium oxide. This is done by dipping the aluminium into sodium hydroxide solution.
- The exposed aluminium is made the **anode** in the electrolysis of dilute sulphuric acid:

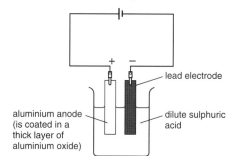

- The oxygen gas made reacts with the aluminium anode. It makes a thicker, protective layer of aluminium oxide.

► Steel making

Iron from the blast furnace contains impurities. Most of these are removed when converting this iron into steel. Oxygen gas is blown over a molten mixture of iron (which includes scrap iron). The impurities get oxidised and are released as gases or removed as slag (formed by adding lime).

There are different types of steel depending on the amount of carbon left in it:
- **High carbon steels** are strong but brittle.
- Whereas **mild steel** (containing less carbon) makes a softer steel that is easy to press into shapes, for example in car bodies.
- **Alloy steels** are made by mixing other metals into the molten steel.

► Electroplating metals

Most metals can be coated with a layer of another metal in an electrolysis cell:

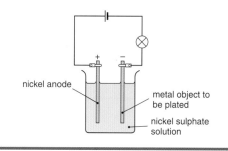

► Extracting titanium

We find titanium in many alloys mixed with other metals. It is used to make low density alloys that can withstand high temperatures. These alloys also resist corrosion. They are used in the aircraft industry, for example, to make the turbines in jet engines.

Titanium is a metal of 'medium' reactivity, so in theory we could use carbon to extract it. However, titanium carbide would be formed which spoils the useful properties of the metal.

> Therefore, we use a ***more reactive metal*** to extract the titanium. In industry sodium or magnesium are used as the reducing agent.

This is the way we extract titanium from its ore:
- Titanium dioxide (TiO_2, rutile) is separated from the ore called ilmenite, which also contains iron oxide, using magnets.
- Titanium dioxide is changed into titanium(IV) chloride ($TiCl_4$):

$$TiO_2(s) \ + \ C(s) \ + \ 2Cl_2(g) \ \xrightarrow{heat} \ TiCl_4(g) \ + \ CO_2(g)$$

- The products are cooled down and titanium(IV) chloride condenses to a liquid. It is purified by distilling it.
- The titanium(IV) chloride is reduced by sodium in an atmosphere of argon:

$$TiCl_4(g) \ + \ 4Na(l) \ \xrightarrow{heat} \ Ti(s) \ + \ 4NaCl(l)$$

- The molten sodium chloride (or magnesium chloride) is tapped off.

We can both reduce titanium chloride.

More in ***Chemistry for You,*** pages, 92, 94, 97, 108, 114 and 154–5.

Examination Questions – Industrial processes

1 Sulphuric acid

This question is about the process by which the element sulphur is turned into sulphuric acid. The first stage in the process is the burning of sulphur in air to give sulphur dioxide:

a) Write a word equation for this reaction.

.... + ... ⟶ ....

(2 marks)

b) The sulphur dioxide SO_2 is then turned into sulphur trioxide SO_3 by heating it with more oxygen in the presence of a vanadium(V) oxide catalyst. The equation for this reaction is shown below.

   i Put numbers in front of the formulae, where necessary, to balance it.

   ....SO_2(g) + ...O_2(g) ⇌ ....SO_3(g)

   ii What does the ⇌ symbol mean?

   ....

(3 marks)

c) The final reaction involves the addition of water to the sulphur trioxide in order to make sulphuric acid.
   Write a symbol equation for this reaction.

   ....

(2 marks)

d) What is the sulphuric acid produced then used for?

   ....

   ....

(2 marks)   9

2 Extracting Titanium

Titanium is one of the transition metals and a metal of medium reactivity. It is extracted from its oxide, TiO_2. Several stages are involved in the process

a) Why is titanium such a useful metal?

   ....

(1 mark)

b) The extraction process is described below.
   Use words from the list to complete the passage:

   reduced, chlorine, carbon, cooled, distillation

   Titanium dioxide is separated from the ore called ilmenite, which also contains iron oxide,

   using magnets. The TiO_2 is heated with .... and ....

   This produces titanium chloride and carbon dioxide gas. The products are then

   .... and the titanium chloride condenses to a liquid. This liquid is

   purified by .... The titanium chloride is then .... by

   sodium metal in an atmosphere of argon.   *(3 marks)*

c) An equation for the last stage in this process is given below:

.................TiCl$_4$(g) + ...Na(l) $\longrightarrow$ .... Ti(s) + ...NaCl(l)

  i Put numbers in front of the formulae, where necessary, in order to balance the equation.

  ii Explain why this reaction can be regarded as a redox reaction.

....

....

(4 marks)   <u>8</u>

3 Making steel

This question is about the way in which iron from the blast furnace is converted to steel.

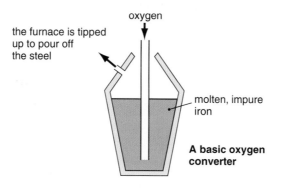

oxygen

the furnace is tipped up to pour off the steel

molten, impure iron

A basic oxygen converter

In this process oxygen is blown through the molten iron. Carbon is one of the impurities.

a) i How does the oxygen remove carbon from the iron?

....

....

  ii Write an equation to represent this reaction.

....

(3 marks)

b) Other metals might be added to the molten iron at this point to make alloys.

  i What is an alloy?

....

  ii Why are alloys useful?

....

(3 marks)   <u>6</u>

1 What is the source of the energy that drives the water cycle?

2 What do we call the type of water that forms a scum with soap?

3 What is the main source of nitrate pollution in water?

4 Which statement is true:

A Most solids get more soluble in water as the temperature rises, but most gases get less soluble.

B Most solids get less soluble in water as the temperature rises, but most gases get more soluble.

► **The water cycle**

Water is a good **solvent**. It forms **solutions** with many **solutes**.

The 'water cycle' shows how water moves around the Earth.

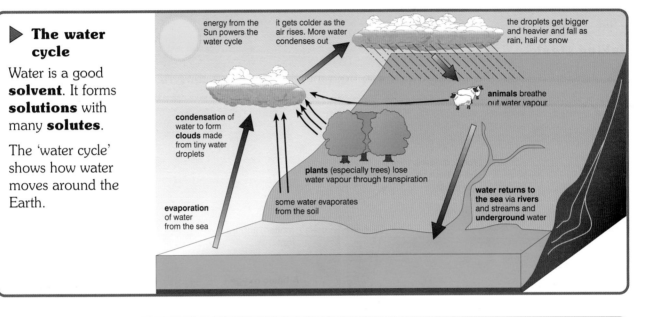

energy from the Sun powers the water cycle

it gets colder as the air rises. More water condenses out

the droplets get bigger and heavier and fall as rain, hail or snow

condensation of water to form **clouds** made from tiny water droplets

animals breathe out water vapour

plants (especially trees) lose water vapour through transpiration

evaporation of water from the sea

some water evaporates from the soil

water returns to the sea via **rivers** and streams and **underground** water

► **Hard water**

Drinking water is purified by **physical** means (filter beds of sand and gravel to remove solids) and **chemical** means (chlorine to kill bacteria) before it reaches our taps.

> **Hard water** contains dissolved **calcium** ions (Ca^{2+}(aq)) and/or **magnesium** ions (Mg^{2+}(aq)).

We can soften the water by **precipitating** these ions out of solution:

calcium ions(aq) + sodium carbonate(aq)

⟶ calcium carbonate(s) + sodium ions(aq)

Or we can soften hard water by passing it through an **ion exchange column**.

Soapless detergents, made from crude oil products, will form lather even in hard water.

Disadvantages of hard water	Advantages of hard water
Difficult to form lather with soap.	Some people prefer the taste.
Scum forms in a reaction which wastes soap.	Calcium in the water is good for children's teeth and bones.
Scale (a hard crust) forms inside kettles. This wastes energy when you boil your kettle.	Helps to reduce heart illness.
	Some brewers like hard water for making beer.
Hot water pipes 'fur up' on the inside. The scale formed can even block up pipes completely.	A coating of scale (limescale) inside copper or lead pipes stops poisonous salts dissolving into our water.

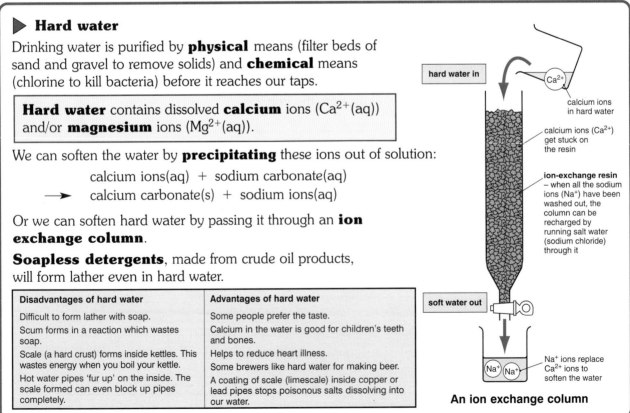

hard water in

calcium ions in hard water

calcium ions (Ca^{2+}) get stuck on the resin

ion-exchange resin – when all the sodium ions (Na^+) have been washed out, the column can be recharged by running salt water (sodium chloride) through it

soft water out

Na^+ ions replace Ca^{2+} ions to soften the water

An ion exchange column

▶ Water pollution

Water is also used as a **coolant** in industry. For example, it takes heat energy away from exothermic reactions in the Contact process used to manufacture sulphuric acid. It also transfers heat in power stations. If hot water that has been used as a coolant is pumped out into rivers it causes **thermal pollution** of the habitat. The delicate balance of nature is disturbed and aquatic life suffers. For example, the hotter the water, the less oxygen gas dissolves in it.

Rivers are also affected by fertilisers, detergents and sewage. Once dissolved into the water, algae thrive. When these die, micro-organisms in the river multiply rapidly as they feed on the dead algae. The micro-organisms use up the dissolved oxygen in the water so aquatic life dies. This problem is called **eutrophication**.

There are also worries about human health as nitrate fertilisers in drinking water are linked with stomach cancer and blue baby disease (where babies are deprived of oxygen).

▶ Solubility curves

Unlike gases, the solubility of most solids increases as we raise the temperature. We can show this on solubility curves:

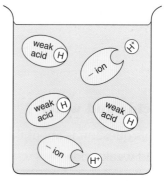

I take no chances with all these nitrates and phosphates nowadays!

▶ Water and acids

For acids to show their acidic properties, water must be present. This is because only when the acids are in solution, can their molecules split up (ionise) to form **$H^+(aq)$ ions**. It is the $H^+(aq)$ ions – protons surrounded by water molecules – that give an acidic solution its characteristic properties:

$$HCl(g) \longrightarrow H^+(aq) + Cl^-(aq)$$

Whereas excess $H^+(aq)$ ions cause acidity in a solution, an excess of hydroxide ions, **$OH^-(aq)$**, cause a solution to be alkaline.

> Acids are said to be proton (H^+) **donors,** whereas bases are proton **acceptors**.

- If almost all the acidic molecules in a solution split up (**complete ionisation**), we call the acid a **strong acid**. Examples include hydrochloric acid, nitric acid and sulphuric acid.
- On the other hand, only a few of the molecules of **weak acids**, such as citric acid, ethanoic acid and carbonic acid, split up in a solution.

Therefore given solutions of equal concentration, a strong acid will have a lower pH value than a weak acid. The strong acid will also react faster than a weak acid, for example with magnesium ribbon, because there is a higher concentration of $H^+(aq)$ ions in its solution.

Solutions of weak acids contain 'undissociated' molecules in equilibrium with H^+ ions and negative ions

More in *Chemistry for You,* pages 149, 238, 250, 296–308.

Answers: **1** the Sun   **2** hard water   **3** nitrate fertilisers   **4** A

Examination Questions – Aqueous chemistry

1 Solubility curves

The diagram opposite shows how the solubility of some solids varies as the temperature is changed.

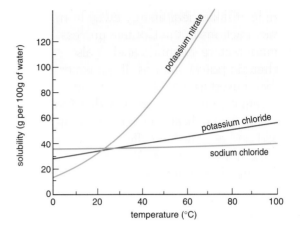

a) What can you say about how the solubility of these solids depends upon temperature ?

....

Marks

(1 mark)

b) What can you say about the effect temperature has upon the solubility of potassium nitrate compared with its effect on the solubility of sodium chloride?

....

....

(2 marks)

Use the data shown on the graph to answer the following questions:

c) i What mass of sodium chloride will dissolve in 100 g water 0°C?

.... *(1 mark)*

ii To what temperature would you need to raise 100 g water in order to dissolve 100 g potassium nitrate in it?

.... *(1 mark)*

iii If the solution produced in ii was cooled to 20°C, what would you expect to see in the tube?

.... *(1 mark)*

6

2 Acids and water

This question is about the differences between strong and weak acids

The diagrams show two test tubes, each containing a different acid.

Both acids are the same concentration. The same amount of magnesium ribbon was placed simultaneously in each tube.

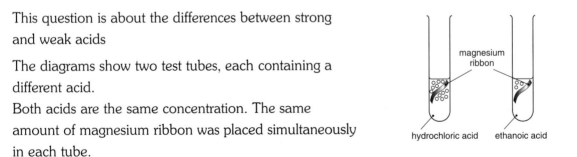

a) What difference can you see between the reactions in the two tubes?

.... *(1 mark)*

b) What does this reaction show about the reactivity of the two acids?

.... *(1 mark)*

c) Explain, using ideas of dynamic equilibrium why this difference exists between the two acids.

....

....

(2 marks) 4

3 **Hard water**

This question is about impurities which are often present in some water supplies.

a) In some areas of the country the water which is supplied to homes and industry is described as 'hard' water.

Use the list below to complete the following passage. Each word should be used once:

calcium carbonate, carbonic acid, magnesium, soluble, calcium

Water which has either calcium or .... ions dissolved in it is

described as hard water. This can form when a river flows over an area where the rock

type is gypsum (which is calcium sulphate). This compound is slightly

... in water and so the .... ions get into the water.

Limestone (which is mainly ....) is not soluble in water but will

dissolve due to the action of ...., formed when carbon dioxide in

the atmosphere is dissolved in rainwater.

(5 marks)

b) Outline two of the disadvantages associated with hard water.

....

.... *(2 marks)*

c) What is meant by

i temporary hardness?

.... *(1 mark)*

ii permanent hardness?

.... *(1 mark)*

d) Explain one way in which permanent hardness can be removed from water.

....

....

....

.... *(2 marks)* 11

19   Detection and identification

▶ **ThinkAbout:**

1 Do the atoms of metals form positively or negatively charged ions?
2 What is the formula of an aluminium ion (Al is in Group 3 in the Periodic Table)?
3 Name three halide ions.
4 What is the charge on a sulphate ion?
5 Give the formula of:
   a) ammonium sulphate   b) iron(III) nitrate.

▶ **Identifying negatively charged ions (anions)**

Here is a summary of the tests we can use to identify some common negatively charged ions (anions):

Anion	Test
Chloride (Cl^-)	Dissolve in dilute nitric acid, then a white precipitate forms with silver nitrate solution. (The precipitate of silver chloride dissolves in dilute ammonia solution.)
Bromide (Br^-) **H**	Dissolve in dilute nitric acid, then a cream precipitate forms with silver nitrate solution. (The precipitate of silver bromide is insoluble in dilute ammonia solution, but dissolves in concentrated ammonia solution.)
Iodide (I^-) **H**	Dissolve in dilute nitric acid, then a pale yellow precipitate forms with silver nitrate solution. (The precipitate of silver iodide is insoluble in both dilute and concentrated ammonia solutions.)
Sulphate (SO_4^{2-})	Dissolve in dilute hydrochloric acid, then a white precipitate of barium sulphate forms with barium chloride solution.
Nitrate (NO_3^-) **H**	Add sodium hydroxide solution and heat, then test the gas given off (ammonia) with damp red litmus paper, which turns blue.
Carbonate (CO_3^{2-})	Add dilute acid, then pass the carbon dioxide gas through limewater, which turns milky (cloudy).

▶ **Identifying positively charged ions (cations)**

Here are the positive ions (cations) we can test with sodium hydroxide solution:

Cation	Result of adding sodium hydroxide solution
Copper(II)	Pale blue precipitate
Iron(II)	Dirty green precipitate
Iron(III)	Rusty brown precipitate
Aluminium	White precipitate which dissolves in excess sodium hydroxide
Magnesium	White precipitate
Calcium	White precipitate

▶ **Flame tests**

Some metal ions also give out coloured light when we heat them in a Bunsen flame:

Cation	Colour of flame test
Sodium	Bright yellow
Lithium	Red (scarlet)
Calcium	Brick red
Potassium	Lilac
Barium	Apple green

H

▶ **Ammonium ions** (NH_4^+) give off ammonia gas when we heat them with sodium hydroxide solution. Ammonia is the only common alkaline gas – we test for ammonia with damp pink litmus paper: it turns blue.

Answers: **1** positively charged ions   **2** Al^{3+} **3** fluoride / chloride / bromide / iodide   **4** 2−   **5** a) $(NH_4)_2SO_4$ b) $Fe(NO_3)_3$

86

▶ Instrumental analysis

Nowadays we can use modern instruments to detect and measure very small amounts of elements and compounds in samples. These machines are used to monitor and control water quality, but have also found many other uses, for example in forensic science and in hospitals. Here is one machine we use to detect unknown elements (in, say, a sample of water being analysed) and one that detects unknown compounds.

▶ Atomic spectrometers

Spectrometers are expensive machines that analyse the energy (in the form of electromagnetic radiation, such as light) absorbed or given out by a sample. Atomic spectrometers are used to detect which elements are in a sample. The sample is heated in a flame. Any molecules are broken down at this stage. The energy from the flame causes electrons in the atoms of the sample to jump into higher energy levels (shells). When the electrons fall back to lower energy levels they give out energy.

The energy given out is called the **emission spectrum** of the element. Each element has its own characteristic set of energies that it gives out. We can see these as lines in a spectrum or as peaks when analysed by a detector and fed into a computer.

This method can be used to tell us which elements are present by matching the emission spectrum to a database of known elements stored on the computer. It can also show how much of each element is present. For example, we can now detect toxic mercury in a sample of water down to traces as low as 0.000 000 001 g!

Atomic spectrometers are used in other industries, besides the water industry, to monitor samples. For example, the steel industry can carefully analyse the amounts of trace elements present in steel to control its quality.

▶ Visible–ultraviolet spectrophotometers

These instruments are used to analyse which compounds are present in a sample. The sample is not broken up by any harsh treatment in the machine, such as heating it in a flame. Light is shone on the sample, then the result is analysed to see which wavelengths are absorbed.

The spectrum can be matched or 'fingerprinted' against known samples and then the sample identified.

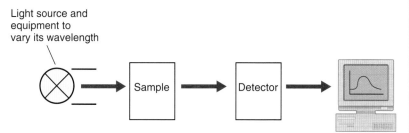

Light source and equipment to vary its wavelength

If a compound does not absorb light in the visible–ultraviolet part of the spectrum, this technique will not work. However, the compound can be reacted with other compounds to give products that do absorb light in the right range. Then these compounds can be detected. This method is used in the water industry to analyse levels of nitrate and phosphate pollutants in water supplies.

▶ Two tell-tale carbonates

- You can recognise **copper carbonate** because it turns from green to black (forming copper oxide) when heated.
- Heating **zinc carbonate** turns the white powder bright yellow. Then it goes white again when cool. It forms zinc oxide, when heated, which is responsible for the colour change.

More in *Chemistry for You,* pages 152–3, 309–11.

Getting the Grades – Triple Award

Try this question, then compare your answer with the two examples opposite ▶

1 This question is about calculating the amounts of substances which are produced when a chemical reaction takes place.

The apparatus shown can be used to decompose samples of solid carbonates.

The equation below shows the reaction which takes place when copper carbonate is heated:

$$CuCO_3(s) \longrightarrow CuO(s) + CO_2(g)$$

(Relative atomic masses: Cu = 64; O = 16; C = 12)

(1 mole of any gas occupies 24 000 cm^3 at 20 °C)

carbonate being tested

limewater

heat

a) Calculate the formula mass of:

   i Copper carbonate, $CuCO_3$

   .... (1 mark)

   ii Copper oxide, CuO

   .... (1 mark)

   iii Carbon dioxide, CO_2

   .... (1 mark)

b) Use your answers to the above questions to calculate the mass of copper oxide which could be produced from 200 g of copper carbonate . Show your workings carefully.

....

....

.... (3 marks)

c) If a student was to perform the same reaction in the laboratory using 12.4 g of copper carbonate, what volume of carbon dioxide would it be possible to obtain at 20 °C?
Show your workings carefully.

....

....

.... (3 marks)

d) Another compound of copper is composed of 47.4% copper and 52.6% chlorine by mass.
(Relative atomic masses: Cu = 64; Cl = 35.5)

Use the information above to calculate the formula of this compound.
Show your workings carefully.

....

....

.... (3 marks)

[Total 12 marks]

1 a) i Copper carbonate, $CuCO_3$ – formula mass : $64 + 12 + (3 \times 16) = 124$ ✓

   ii Copper oxide, CuO – formula mass : $64 + 16 = 80$ ✓

   iii Carbon dioxide, CO_2 – formula mass : $12 + (16 \times 2) = 44$ ✓

  b) $CuCO_3(s) \rightarrow CuO(s) + CO_2(g)$

      124 g   :   80 g   ✓

      1   :   124/80   ✗——————

      200   :   200 × (124/80) = 310

      mass of copper oxide produced = 310 g ✗

  c) Mass of $CuCO_3(s)$ = 12.4. No. of Moles = 12.4/124 = 0.1 ✓

      From the equation : $CuCO_3(s) \rightarrow CuO(s) + CO_2(g)$

      Number of moles of carbon dioxide produced = 0.1 ✓

      Volume of carbon dioxide produced = $0.1 \times 24000 = 2400\ cm^3$ ✓

The candidate has made an error calculating the mass of CuO made from 1 g of $CuCO_3$. It should be 80 divided by 124, i.e. (80/124 g).

  d)

Considering 100g of the compound	Copper	Chlorine
Mass/g	47.4	52.6 ✓
No. moles	47.4/64 = 0.74	52.6/35.5 = 1.48 ✓
Simplest ratio	0.74/0.74 = 1	1.48/0.74 = 2
	= 1 :	2
Formula		$CuCl_2$ ✓

10 marks = Grade A answer

► **Improve your Grades   A up to A***

When tackling questions like this take care to use formulae and equations wherever possible to organise your calculations. It is absolutely vital to set out your workings with care in this sort of question. The two column format used in d) is common when trying to convert masses of percentages into a chemical formula. Learn this as a standard technique.

Where you can, use chemical formula and equations to help organise your thoughts and your answers.

1 a) i Copper carbonate, $CuCO_3$ – formula mass : $64 + 12 + (3 \times 16) = 124$ ✓

   ii Copper oxide, CuO – formula mass : $64 + 16 = 80$ ✓

   iii Carbon dioxide, CO_2 – formula mass : $12 + 16 = 28$ ✗

  b) $CuCO_3(s) \rightarrow CuO(s) + CO_2(g)$

      124 g   →   80 g   ✓

           ✗ ✗

The candidate has performed the first step correctly but stopped there.

The last step has been missed out

  c) Mass of $CuCO_3(s)$ = 12.4. No. of Moles = 12.4/124 = 0.1 ✓

      From the equation: $CuCO_3(s) \rightarrow CuO(s) + CO_2(g)$

      Number of moles of carbon dioxide produced = 0.1 ✓

The candidate has failed to convert the number of moles to a ratio and therefore a formula.

  d)

Considering 100g of the compound	Copper	Chlorine
Mass/g	47.4	52.6 ✓
No. moles	47.4/64 = 0.74	52.6/35.5 = 1.48 ✓

7 marks = Grade C answer

► **Improve your Grades   C up to B**

Spend some time practising the calculation of formula masses. Where there is a subscript number after the symbol of an element, the atomic mass must be multiplied by that number to include its contribution to the formula mass. Use brackets to help you with these calculations – and, as ever, set out your workings clearly.

Examination answers and tips ✓

TOPIC 1. Atomic structure

1 a) A = electron, B = neutron, C = proton

b) B

c)   i 3   ii 3+   iii 27   **7**

2 a) 15   b) 16   c) 15   **3**

3 a)   i

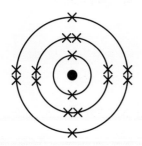

ii 32   iii S

b) Neutron

c) They contain the same number of protons (+) and electrons (−).   **5**

TOPIC 2. Bonding

1 a) X is an ion ('atom' is acceptable)
Y is an electron

b) The atoms in metals are organised in a regular fashion in layers. Because of this, layers can, when subjected to external forces, slip easily over one another, allowing the metal to bend.

c) The atoms (or ions) are bonded together by a 'sea' of free electrons. The free electrons can drift through the metal (giant lattice) when a voltage is applied.   **6**

Examiner's Tip ✓
The idea of a regular arrangement of atoms in a giant metallic lattice is important as it helps to explain many of the properties of metals.

2 a) $2\,Mg + O_2 \longrightarrow 2\,MgO$

b)   i   ii

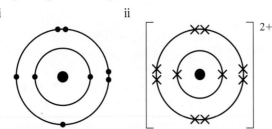

c) Ionic substances are made up of oppositely charged ions which attract one another in order to form an interlocking giant lattice. A lot of energy is needed to break up such a lattice and therefore it has a high melting point.

d) On descending the group, the atom of each successive element has an additional electron shell. This results in the electrons in the outermost shells becoming further from the nucleus and therefore more easily removed. Since metals react by losing their outer electrons, the elements lower down the group react more vigorously.   **9**

Examiner's Tip ✓
This change in the number of electron shells is also the reason the reactivity of the halogens decreases down the group. It gets more difficult for the halogen atoms to attract an extra electron into their outer shell the further it is from the attractive force of the nucleus.

TOPIC 3. Useful products from oil

1 a) hydrocarbons

b) evaporation, condensation, distillation

c) lower, more

d)   i e.g. packing/bags/bottles/buckets

ii The material can be broken down and decomposed by the action of natural processes such the action of microbes in the soil

iii Polythene does not biodegrade and so will take up space in landfill sites. Disposal by burning produces large amounts of atmospheric pollution.   **9**

Examiner's Tip ✓
Plastics can be made biodegradeable – but they are more expensive.

2 a) Alkanes are compounds whose molecules are composed of atoms of hydrogen and carbon only. All the bonds in an alkane are single bonds. Each carbon atom bonds to four other atoms, and each hydrogen atom bonds to only one carbon atom. The number of hydrogen atoms in a given alkane molecule will therefore depend upon the number of carbon atoms in the molecule – this is given by the formula C_nH_{2n+2}.

Examiner's Tip ✓
The Alkanes are a 'family' of compounds which share the same general formula. Knowing the number of carbon atoms (n) enables you to work out the molecular formula for any particular alkane.

b) Polymerisation takes place when thousands of small, reactive molecules (monomers) join up with one another to form a large molecule (polymer). Therefore a polymer is made up of a large number of identical repeating units. **5**

TOPIC 4. Useful products from metal ores

1 a) 70 % of the ore is iron oxide. Thus in 2000 tonnes (of ore) the amount (mass) of iron oxide is

$$\left(\frac{2000}{100}\right) \times 70 = 1400 \text{ tonnes}$$

b) Formula of iron oxide is Fe_2O_3

The formula mass of iron oxide is $(2 \times 56) + (3 \times 16) = 160$

The proportion of iron in iron oxide is $\frac{112}{160}$

Thus the mass of iron that can be extracted from 1400 tonnes iron oxide is thus $\left(\frac{112}{160}\right) \times 1400$ = 980 tonnes **4**

2 a) Ionic compounds have high melting points because the oppositely charged ions are attracted strongly to one another, and a rigid three dimensional lattice is formed as a result.

b)

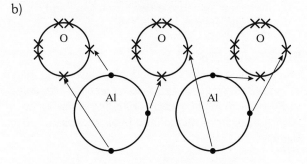

c) $Al^{3+} + 3\ e^- \longrightarrow Al$ **5**

3 a) i limestone

ii hot air

iii Molten slag

b) i $Fe_2O_3(s) + 3CO(g) \longrightarrow 2Fe(l) + 3CO_2(g)$

ii Iron oxide has been reduced

c) i Formula mass = $(56 \times 2) + (3 \times 16) = 160$

ii Percentage of iron in iron oxide

$= \left(\frac{112}{160}\right) \times 100 = 70\%$

iii Mass of iron in 1000 kg iron oxide

$= 1000 \times \left(\frac{70}{100}\right) = 700 \text{ kg}$ **10**

TOPIC 5. Useful products from rocks and air

1 a) Iron is used as a catalyst to speed up the reaction.

b) nitrogen + hydrogen $\rightleftharpoons$ ammonia

c) i The reaction is reversible and so some of the ammonia which form splits up to form nitrogen and hydrogen.

ii The mixture of ammonia, nitrogen and hydrogen is cooled. This causes the ammonia gas to liquefy (condense) and separate from the unreacted hydrogen and nitrogen.
The unreacted hydrogen and nitrogen are recycled into the converter. **5**

2 a) Air

  b) i Platinum

   ii Oxidation

  c) i nitric acid + **potassium hydroxide**
     $\longrightarrow$ potassium nitrate + **water**

   ii Fertiliser

   iii H$^+$ 7

3 a) top left – carbon dioxide
    top right – calcium carbonate
    bottom – calcium oxide

  b) Thermal decomposition   5

TOPIC 6. Representing reactions

1 a) i lead oxide + carbon $\longrightarrow$ carbon dioxide + lead

   ii 44

Examiner's Tip ✓
Note that mass is conserved. The total mass after reaction is equal to the total mass before reaction.

  b) i carbon dioxide + carbon $\longrightarrow$ carbon monoxide

   ii $C(s) + O_2(g) \longrightarrow CO_2(g)$

   iii $Fe_2O_3(s) + 3CO(g) \longrightarrow 2Fe(l) + 3CO_2(g)$ 7

Examiner's Tip ✓
Note that each carbon monoxide combines with one oxygen. Thus in order to remove 3 oxygens from the iron, 3 carbon monoxides are required.

2 a) i copper chloride $\longrightarrow$ copper + chlorine

   ii $Cu^{2+}(aq) + 2e^- \longrightarrow Cu(s)$

   iii $2Cl^-(aq) \longrightarrow Cl_2(g) + 2e^-$ 5

Examiner's Tip ✓
*Remember: **O**xidation **is l**oss, reduction **is g**ain*
and
*Redu**C**tion takes place at the **C**athode, oxid**a**tion at the **a**node*

TOPIC 7. Changes to the Earth and atmosphere

1 a) 1. There is much less carbon dioxide in the Earth's atmosphere

   2. There is much more nitrogen (78%) in the Earth's atmosphere

   3. Oxygen is present in the Earth's atmosphere (21%)

  b) Green plants can use light energy to photosynthesise. This process uses up carbon dioxide and releases oxygen   5

Examiner's Tip ✓
Although there is concern about the effect of rising levels of carbon dioxide in the atmosphere, the percentage is still very small indeed (approx 0.04%)

2 a) The amount of carbon dioxide in the atmosphere has risen over the last 300 years. The rate of increase has itself increased steadily over this time period.

  b) The change in the amount of carbon dioxide in the atmosphere is caused partly by the **burning** of **fuels**. One effect of this change in the amount of carbon dioxide is the increase in the **temperature** of the atmosphere.   5

Examiner's Tip ✓
The destruction of rainforests also contributes to the rising carbon dioxide levels.

3 a) The modern atmosphere is composed mainly of **nitrogen** which is a very **unreactive** gas. This was produced partly as a result of the action of **bacteria** in the soil which **decompose** nitrates in the soil. The reactive gas **oxygen** which is essential for life was produced as a result of **photosynthesis** by green plants.

  b) i It has decreased

   ii When exposed to light, green plants photosynthesise using up carbon dioxide. Carbon dioxide also dissolves in seawater – and is used in the formation of the shells of sea creatures

  c) i The burning of fossil fuels has led to an increase in the carbon dioxide levels in the atmosphere

   ii They think it is leading to global warming which may cause a rise in sea level and flooding in low lying areas.   10

Examiner's Tip ✓
Other problems associated with global warming might include more frequent extremes of weather; droughts and floods; changing patterns of crop production; extinction of some animal and plant species as habitats change.

TOPIC 8. The rock record

1 a) i X is the mantle
Y is the inner core

ii Since the overall density of the Earth is so large, the material in the lower layers of the Earth must be much more (approximately 2 ×) dense than the material which makes up the Earth's crust.

b) A land bridge would have enabled animals to migrate between South America and Africa and so their fossils would be likely to be found on both continents. The disappearance of the land bridge would leave these animals isolated from one another and therefore able to evolve differently.

c) i Major earthquakes tend to take place along plate boundaries. Britain does not lie on a plate boundary and therefore does not have major earthquakes

ii The material in the mantle is circulating under the influence of convection currents. The heat is generated by radioactive atoms in the mantle beneath the plates.

d) i The crust and upper part of the mantle.

ii iron and nickel

iii solid **14**

Examiner's Tip ✓

Comment: Be careful in questions like this to note the number of marks being awarded and to be sure to make the corresponding number of points in your answers.

Higher Tier only: Note that in the theory of plate tectonics further evidence for the moving apart of plates is also available in the magnetic banding shown in regions such the mid Atlantic ridge.

TOPIC 9. Chemical calculations

1 a) Al_2O_3 – Formula mass = $(27 \times 2) + (16 \times 3)$
$= 54 + 48 = 102$

b) % aluminium = $(54/ 102) \times 100 = 53\%$

c) Mass of aluminium in 1000 kg of aluminium oxide
$= 1000 \times (53/100) = 530$ kg **6**

Examiner's Tip ✓

Be sure to show all your working out in calculations like these.

2 a) $CuFeS_2$ – Formula mass = $64 + 56 + (32 \times 2)$
$= 184$

b) % by mass of copper in copper pyrites
$= \left(\dfrac{64}{184} \right) \times 100$
$= 34.8 \%$ **3**

3 Fomula masses:
$H_2SO_4 = (2 \times 1) + 32 + (4 \times 16) = 98$
$CaCO_3 = 40 + 12 + (3 \times 16) = 100$
From the equation sulphuric acid reacts with calcium carbonate in a ratio of 1:1

Therefore 98 g of sulphuric acid is neutralised by 100 g of calcium carbonate

98 tonnes of sulphuric acid is neutralised by 100 tonnes of calcium carbonate

1 tonne of sulphuric acid is neutralised by
$\dfrac{100}{98}$ tonnes of calcium carbonate

4900 tonne of sulphuric acid is neutralised by
$\left(\dfrac{100}{98} \right) \times 4900 = 5000$ tonnes of calcium carbonate **3**

Examiner's Tip ✓

This sort of calculation can be set out in different ways and still be correct. Note that you should show a series of logical steps in order to get full marks.

4

	nitrogen	oxygen
mass /g	0.56	0.32
no. moles	0.56/14	0.32/16
	0.040	0.020

Ratio of moles 2 : 1

Therefore the formula of the nitrogen oxide is N_2O **4**

Examiner's Tip ✓

It is very important in this type of question to set out your workings with care. A simple table like that used above is often helpful.

TOPIC 10. The Periodic Table

1 a) i Y   ii W   iii X   iv Z

b) Group 7, the Halogens, and Group 0 the Noble
gases   **5**

2 a) The atomic number of the element

b) In the modern periodic table the vertical columns
contain elements with similar electronic structures
which therefore have similar properties to one
another. This is more useful as it enables predictions
about an element's behaviour to be made.

   i Ca

   ii Ne

   iii Cs

   iv P

   v Am, Fm, Ha   **7**

TOPIC 11. Acids, alkalis and salts

1 a)   i Solution B

   ii Solution D

   iii Solution A

   i Neutral

   ii Neutralisation

2

Acid	Alkali	Salt	Formula of salt
Hydrochloric acid	Sodium hydroxide	Sodium chloride	$NaCl$
Nitric acid	Sodium hydroxide	**Sodium nitrate**	$NaNO_3$
Sulphuric acid	Potassium hydroxide	**Potassium sulphate**	K_2SO_4

      4

3 a) A conical flask

b) Hydrogen gas

c) Magnesium chloride

d) magnesium + hydrochloric acid
     ➤ magnesium chloride + hydrogen

e) i Add more magnesium ribbon until no more will
dissolve, and a small excess remains in the flask

   ii Filter the contents of the flask into an
evaporating basin. Heat the evaporating basin
on a water bath to evaporate some water from
the solution. Continue until the solution is
sufficiently saturated to crystallise on cooling

f) Nitric acid   **10**

TOPIC 12. Rates of reaction

1 a) There will be a steeper curve initially, which levels off
at the same point (volume of hydrogen).

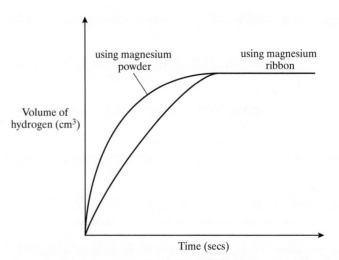

b) In a more concentrated acid there will be more
particles of acid in a given volume and therefore
more collisions will take place between particles of
acid and particles of magnesium in a given time.

c) magnesium + hydrochloric acid
→ magnesium chloride + hydrogen   **6**

2 a) The rate of carbon dioxide production decreases as the reaction proceeds. This is because as the acid get used up, its concentration decreases and there are fewer collisions per second between the acid and the calcium carbonate. The graph levels off at 83 cm^3 when all the acid has been used up and no more gas can be produced.

b) The new curve will be steeper initially and will level off at the same point (volume of carbon dioxide).

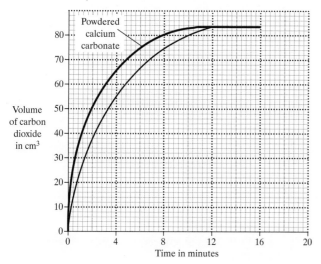

c) Changing the temperature, using an acid of different concentration and using a catalyst, will all change the rate of the reaction. (Any one of these suggestions will get the mark)   **5**

TOPIC 13. Enzymes

1 a) In beer-making yeast converts *sugar* into carbon dioxide and *alcohol*.
In yoghurt-making, bacteria convert *milk sugar* into *lactic acid*.

b) The gas is bubbled through limewater. If the limewater becomes cloudy (ie a white precipitiate forms), the gas is carbon dioxide.   **6**

2 a) Alcohol produced in this way is used in making *wine*. Carbon dioxide produced by fermentation can be used to make *bread* rise.

b) i Enzymes work best at normal temperatures (around body temperature), so heating is not usually required.
   ii If the temperature is increased, the enzyme can be easily damaged and become ineffective.   **4**

3 a) 1. Barley
       2. Water
       3. Hops
       4. Sugar
       5. Maize
   any four of these five will get 2 marks
   any three of these five will get 1 mark

b) The enzyme will speed up the reaction without becoming used up in it.

c) Carbon dioxide gas

d) i Exothermic
   ii If the solution becomes too hot, the enzyme will be denatured and will therefore become ineffective.   **6**

TOPIC 14. Reversible reactions

1 a) The reaction was endothermic.
   Heat needed to be supplied to the reactant in order to break bonds and release the water molecules.

b) i The symbol ⇌ is used to indicate a reversible reaction
   ii The white powder can be turned back to blue by adding water to it   **3**

2 a) The two half headed arrows: $\rightleftharpoons$
are used to represent a dynamic equilibrium

b) The value for ΔH is negative, thus the reaction is exothermic

c) i An increase in pressure favours the side of the reaction with fewer molecules so the equilibrium will move to the right.

ii Since the equilibrium moves to the right, the yield of ammonia will increase.

iii Since the forward reaction is exothermic, the reverse reaction is endothermic. An increase in temperature will therefore favour the reverse reaction, shifting the equilibrium to the left. This will reduce the yield of ammonia.

d) A relatively high temperature is needed in order to achieve an acceptable rate of reaction despite the fact that this reduces the yield.

e) A catalyst will speed up the rate of reaction without becoming used up itself. It will be more effective when finely divided as this increases its surface area. **10**

Examiner's Tip ✓
It is important to note the economic importance of achieving an acceptable rate for industrial processes. The use of a catalyst allows industrial processes to be carried out at a cost effective rate but at lower (and therefore less costly) temperatures.

Remember that a catalyst itself does not affect the position of equilibrium so does not change the percentage yield of product in a reversible reaction.

TOPIC 15. Energy transfer

1 Exothermic
Released as heat **2**

2 a) Energy associated with bonds broken:
$= (1 \times H{-}H) + (1 \times Cl{-}Cl) = 436 + 240 = 676$

Energy associated with new bonds formed:
$= 2 \times H{-}Cl = 2 \times 431 = 862$

Energy exchanged with the surroundings
$= 676 - 862 = -186 \text{ kJ mol}^{-1}$

Examiner's Tip ✓
The energy released by the formation of new bonds is greater than the energy required to break the bond in the reactant molecules and therefore the reaction is exothermic

b)

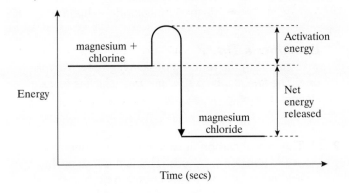

Examiner's Tip ✓
Note that the activation energy needs to be supplied in order to start the reaction. In this case, the energy of the reactants is higher than the energy of the products and thus the reaction is exothermic.

c) Endothermic

d) 125 kJmol^{-1} taken in. **9**

TOPIC 16. Organic chemistry

1 Alcohols

a) i Carbon dioxide

ii glucose $\xrightarrow{\text{yeast}}$ ethanol + carbon dioxide

b) $C_2H_4(g) + H_2O(g) \longrightarrow C_2H_5OH(l)$ or (g)

c) i The process involving ethene can be a continuous process

ii The fermentation process uses a renewable resource.

d) Ethanol can be used as a fuel and as a solvent **8**

Examiner's Tip ✓
The use of ethanol as a fuel has a number of environmental advantages. Ethanol burns with a clean flame and if made from sugar, it makes no overall contribution to global warming.

2 Isomers

a) i Isomer A will have the higher boiling point

ii The straight chain alkane molecules can pack together better and therefore will have stronger forces between the molecules than those of the branched chain alkane.

b) There will be no chemical differences between these two isomers, since they have the same atoms and types of bonds as each other. **5**

Examiner's Tip ✓
Not all isomers will have identical chemical properties – but provided the two isomer have the same functional groups then it is likely they will undergo the same reactions (perhaps at a different rate).

3 Carboxylic acids

a) Ethanoic acid CH_3COOH
   Propanoic acid C_2H_5COOH

b) i The magnesium will dissolve, giving off hydrogen gas, forming a solution of the magnesium (carboxylate) salt

   ii The sodium carbonate solution will effervesce, giving off carbon dioxide gas and a solution of the sodium (carboxylate) salt of the acid.

c) i Esters

   ii alcohols + carboxylic acids $\longrightarrow$ ester + water

d) Esters are used in flavourings and perfumes. **10**

TOPIC 17. Industrial processes

1 Sulphuric acid

a) sulphur + oxygen $\longrightarrow$ sulphur dioxide

b) i $2SO_2(g) + O_2(g) \rightleftharpoons 2SO_3$

   ii The reaction is in a state of dynamic equilibrium

c) $SO_3(g) + H_2O(l) \longrightarrow H_2SO_4(l)$

d) Detergents, fertilisers, car batteries, as a dehydrating agent (any two) **9**

2 Extracting titanium

a) It is used for making strong and corrosion resistant alloys

b) Titanium dioxide is separated from the ore called ilmenite which also contains iron oxide using magnets. The TiO_2 is heated with **carbon** and **chlorine**. This produces titanium chloride and carbon dioxide gas. The products are then **cooled** and the titanium chloride condenses to a liquid. This liquid is purified by **distillation**. The titanium chloride is the **reduced** by sodium metal in an atmosphere of argon.

c) i $TiCl_4(g) + 4Na(l) \longrightarrow Ti(s) + 4NaCl(l)$

   ii The titanium is **Red**uced (gains electrons); the sodium is **ox**idised (loses electrons). Hence reduction and oxidation take place simultaneously **8**

3 Making steel

a) i It combines with the carbon to form carbon dioxide gas which is given off.

   ii $C(s) + O_2(g) \longrightarrow CO_2(g)$

b) i A mixture of two or more metals

   ii The mixing of metals change the way in which the atoms in the metal behave and can give the alloy useful properties such as corrosion resistance and high strength. **6**

TOPIC 18. Aqueous chemistry

1 Solubility curves

a) The solubility of these salts increases as the temperature increases

b) Temperature has a large effect on the solubility of potassium nitrate. The solubility of sodium chloride is only slightly affected by a change in temperature.

c) i $35\,g \pm 1\,g$

   ii $57°C \pm 2°C$

   iii potassium nitrate (white) crystals would appear **6**

2 Acids and water

a) The magnesium reacts more vigorously in the hydrochloric acid

b) The hydrochloric acid is the more reactive of the two acids

c) The hydrochloric acid is a strong acid – this means that all its molecules had ionised to form hydrogen ions. The ethanoic acid is not fully ionised – its molecules are in dynamic equilibrium with its ions. **4**

3 Hard water

a) Water which has either calcium or **magnesium** ions dissolved in it is described as hard water. This can form when a river flows over an area where the rock type is gypsum (which is calcium sulphate). This compound is slightly **soluble** in water and so the **calcium** ions get into the water. Limestone (which is mainly **calcium carbonate**) is not soluble in water but will dissolve due to the action of **carbonic acid**, formed when carbon dioxide in the atmosphere is dissolved in rainwater.

b) Limescale can clog up pipes and heating elements. Hard water will react with soap to produce a scum, making it more difficult to get a lather.

c) i Temporary hardness is hardness which can be removed by boiling

   ii Permanent hardness is hardness which remains even after the water has been boiled

d) *Either:* The water can be passed through an ion exchange resin which exchanges calcium ions for sodium ions.

or: Washing soda (sodium carbonate) is added to the water to precipitate out the calcium ions as calcium carbonate.　　　**11**

TOPIC 19. Detection and identification

Precipitation reactions

1 a) An insoluble solid formed as the result of a reaction taking place in solution.

　b) i silver nitrate + sodium chloride
　　　　　$\longrightarrow$ silver chloride + sodium nitrate

　　ii Silver chloride

　　iii Chloride ions

　c) i Dip a loop of clean wire into pure water then into a sample of the solid to be tested. Put the wire and sample at the tip of the blue cone of a Bunsen Burner flame with the air hole open. Note the colour of the flame produced.

　　ii Bright yellow.　　　**9**

Unknown compound

2 a) Potassium / K^+

　b) Sulphate / SO_4^{2-}

　c) K_2SO_4

　d) $K_2SO_4(aq) + BaCl_2(aq)$
　　　　　$\longrightarrow BaSO_4(s) + 2KCl(aq)$　　　**5**

Identification

3 a) *Reaction 1.* When a sample of copper carbonate was heated in a test tube, its colour changed from a **green** powder to copper oxide which is a **black** powder. Carbon dioxide gas was given off in this process. This gas was identified by the fact that it produced a **white** precipitate when bubbled through limewater.

Reaction 2. When dilute acid was added to a sample of the copper carbonate, bubbles of **colourless** gas were produced.

Reaction 3. The copper oxide produced in 1 was added to dilute nitric acid until no more would dissolve. Excess copper oxide was then filtered out. The resultant solution was tested by the addition of sodium hydroxide solution. This reacted with the metal ions present, to produce a **pale blue** precipitate

　b) Copper carbonate $\longrightarrow$ copper oxide + carbon dioxide
　　Thermal decomposition

　c) Green powder dissolved in colourless liquid to produce bubbles of colourless gas and producing a blue/green solution.

　d) i Neutralisation

　　ii $CuO(s) + 2HNO_3(aq)$
　　　　　$\longrightarrow Cu(NO_3)_2(aq) + H_2O(l)$　　　**10**

Data Sheet

1 Reactivity Series of Metals

Potassium	most reactive
Sodium	
Calcium	
Magnesium	
Aluminium	
Carbon	
Zinc	
Iron	
Tin	
Lead	
Hydrogen	
Copper	
Silver	
Gold	
Platinum	least reactive

(elements in italics, though non-metals, have been included for comparison).

---

2 Formulae of Some Common Ions

Positive ions

Name	Formula
Hydrogen	H^+
Sodium	Na^+
Silver	Ag^+
Potassium	K^+
Lithium	Li^+
Ammonium	NH_4^+
Barium	Ba^{2+}
Calcium	Ca^{2+}
Copper(II)	Cu^{2+}
Magnesium	Mg^{2+}
Zinc	Zn^{2+}
Lead	Pb^{2+}
Iron(II)	Fe^{2+}
Iron(III)	Fe^{3+}
Aluminium	Al^{3+}

Negative ions

Name	Formula
Chloride	Cl^-
Bromide	Br^-
Fluoride	F^-
Iodide	I^-
Hydroxide	OH^-
Nitrate	NO_3^-
Oxide	O^{2-}
Sulphide	S^{2-}
Sulphate	SO_4^{2-}
Carbonate	CO_3^{2-}

3   The Periodic Table of Elements

KEY

Relative atomic mass A_r

Atomic number (Proton number) Z

1		H	
		Hydrogen	
		1	

1	2											3	4	5	6	7	0
																	4 **He** Helium 2
7 **Li** Lithium 3	9 **Be** Beryllium 4											11 **B** Boron 5	12 **C** Carbon 6	14 **N** Nitrogen 7	16 **O** Oxygen 8	19 **F** Fluorine 9	20 **Ne** Neon 10
23 **Na** Sodium 11	24 **Mg** Magnesium 12											27 **Al** Aluminium 13	28 **Si** Silicon 14	31 **P** Phosphorus 15	32 **S** Sulphur 16	35.5 **Cl** Chlorine 17	40 **Ar** Argon 18
39 **K** Potassium 19	40 **Ca** Calcium 20	45 **Sc** Scandium 21	48 **Ti** Titanium 22	51 **V** Vanadium 23	52 **Cr** Chromium 24	55 **Mn** Manganese 25	56 **Fe** Iron 26	59 **Co** Cobalt 27	59 **Ni** Nickel 28	64 **Cu** Copper 29	65 **Zn** Zinc 30	70 **Ga** Gallium 31	73 **Ge** Germanium 32	75 **As** Arsenic 33	79 **Se** Selenium 34	80 **Br** Bromine 35	84 **Kr** Krypton 36
85 **Rb** Rubidium 37	88 **Sr** Strontium 38	89 **Y** Yttrium 39	91 **Zr** Zirconium 40	93 **Nb** Niobium 41	96 **Mo** Molybdenum 42	99 **Tc** Technetium 43	101 **Ru** Ruthenium 44	103 **Rh** Rhodium 45	106 **Pd** Palladium 46	108 **Ag** Silver 47	112 **Cd** Cadmium 48	115 **In** Indium 49	119 **Sn** Tin 50	122 **Sb** Antimony 51	128 **Te** Tellurium 52	127 **I** Iodine 53	131 **Xe** Xenon 54
133 **Cs** Caesium 55	137 **Ba** Barium 56	139 **La** Lanthanum 57	178 **Hf** Hafnium 72	181 **Ta** Tantalum 73	184 **W** Tungsten 74	186 **Re** Rhenium 75	190 **Os** Osmium 76	192 **Ir** Iridium 77	195 **Pt** Platinum 78	197 **Au** Gold 79	201 **Hg** Mercury 80	204 **Tl** Thallium 81	207 **Pb** Lead 82	209 **Bi** Bismuth 83	Po Polonium 84	At Astatine 85	Rn Radon 86
Fr Francium 87	226 **Ra** Radium 88	227 **Ac** Actinium 89															

Elements 58-71 and 90-103 have been omitted.

Index

Published in 2005 by:
Nelson Thornes Ltd
Delta Place
27 Bath Road
CHELTENHAM
GL53 7TH
United Kingdom

05 06 07 08 09 / 10 9 8 7 6 5 4 3 2 1

A catalogue record for this book is available from the British Library

ISBN 0 7487 9588-X

Page make-up by Tech-Set
Printed in Croatia by Zrinski

Acknowledgements

We would like to thank examiners Bob McDuell and David Fowkes for their help
with the examination questions, answers and tips.

AQA acknowledgements

AQA examination questions are reproduced by permission of the Assessment and Qualifications
Alliance.

Chap. 1 Science: Double Award (co-ordinated) Paper 2 – Foundation Tier June 2001 Q2;
Science: Single Award (co-ordinated) Paper 2 – Higher Tier June 2001 Q6; Chap. 2 Science:
Double Award (Modular) – Higher Tier Paper 1 June 2003 Q15; Science: Double Award
(co-ordinated) Paper 2 – Higher Tier June 2001 Q9; Chap. 3 Science Double Award Foundation
Tier June 2003, Q4; Double Award (Modular) – Paper 2 Higher Tier 9 June 2003, Q14;
Chap. 5 Science: Double Award (Modular) Higher Tier – Paper 2 June 2003 Q11; Science:
Double Award (Modular) Higher Tier – Paper 1 June 2003 Q12; Science: Double Award
(co-ordinated) Higher Tier – Paper 2 June 2003 Q4; Chap. 6 Science: Double Award (modular) –
Foundation Tier June 2003 Q16; Science: Single Award (co-ordinated) – Foundation Tier
June 2003 Q3; Chap. 9 Science: Double Award (co-ordinated) Higher Tier – Paper 2 June 2003
Q5; Science: Double Award – (co-ordinated) – Foundation Tier – Paper 2 June 2001 Q3;
Chap. 10 Science: Double Award (co-ordinated) – Foundation Tier – Paper 3 June Q9;
Chap. 11 Science: Double Award (modular) Higher Tier – Paper 1 June 2003 Q4; Science:
Double Award (co-ordinated) Higher Tier – Paper 2 June 2001 Q3; Chap. 12 Science: Single
Award – (modular) – Foundation Tier June 2001 Q20; Year 11– GScience: Double Award
(modular) – Higher Tier – Paper 1 June 2003 Q10; Chap. 15 Science: Single Award (modular) –
Higher Tier June 2001 Q9; Science: Double Award (modular) – Higher Tier – Paper 2 June 2003
Q4; Chap. 16 Science: Single Award (modular) June 2003 Q4; Science: Double Award (modular)
– Foundation Tier – Paper 2 June 2003 Q6; Science: Double Award(co-ordinated) Foundation Tier
– Paper 2 June 2001 Q15; Chap. 17 Science: Double Award (co-ordinated) – Foundation Tier
June 2003 Q9; Chap. 18 Science: Single Award (Modular) – Foundation Tier June 2001 Q7;
Science: Single Award (Modular) June 2001 Q10; Science: Double Award (Modular) June 2003
Q10; Chap. 19 Science: Double Award (co-ordinated) – Foundation Tier June 2003 Q15 c;
Science: Double Award (co-ordinated) June 2001 Q13 e; Science: Double Award (co-ordinated)
Paper 2 – Higher Tier June 2001 Q6 c; Science: Double Award (co-ordinated) Paper 2 – Higher
Tier June 2001 7c

Please note that the following AQA(NEAB) questions used on pages 19, 42, 47, 50, 51, 62, 63,
68, 69, 73, 76–77, 80 are NOT from the live examinations for the current specification.

AQA take no responsibility for answers given to their questions within this publication.

Photograph acknowledgements

Photodisc 18 (NT), p.53.